WANDA

The untold story of
The Wanda Beach Murders

WANDA

The untold story of The Wanda Beach Murders

ALAN J. WHITICKER

First edition published in 2003 by New Holland Publishers
This edition published in 2021 by New Holland Publishers
Sydney • Auckland

Level 1, 178 Fox Valley Road, Wahroonga 2076, Australia
5/39 Woodside Ave, Northcote, Auckland 0627, New Zealand
newhollandpublishers.com

www.newhollandpublishers.com

A record of this book is held at the National Library of Australia.

ISBN 9781760793395

Managing Director: Fiona Schultz
Editor: Alan Whiticker
Designer: Yolanda La Gorcé
Production Director: Arlene Gippert

10 9 8 7 6 5 4 3 2 1

Keep up with New Holland Publishers:

NewHollandPublishers

@newhollandpublishers

All photographs used in the text and on the cover are courtesy of News Ltd.

Cover photographs:
Front Main image: Close friends Christine Sharrock (left) and Marianne
Schmidt (right) were 'inseparable'. Both were fifteen years old when they were
murdered at Wanda Beach on 11 January 1965. Their killer has never been
identified. Background Image: Wanda carpark 1962

Back Cover Image: Sydney detectives examine the crime scene at Wanda Beach
on 12 January 1965. 'The body' is partially exposed in the foreground … 'nature's
grim illusion' that hid the reality of two bodies.

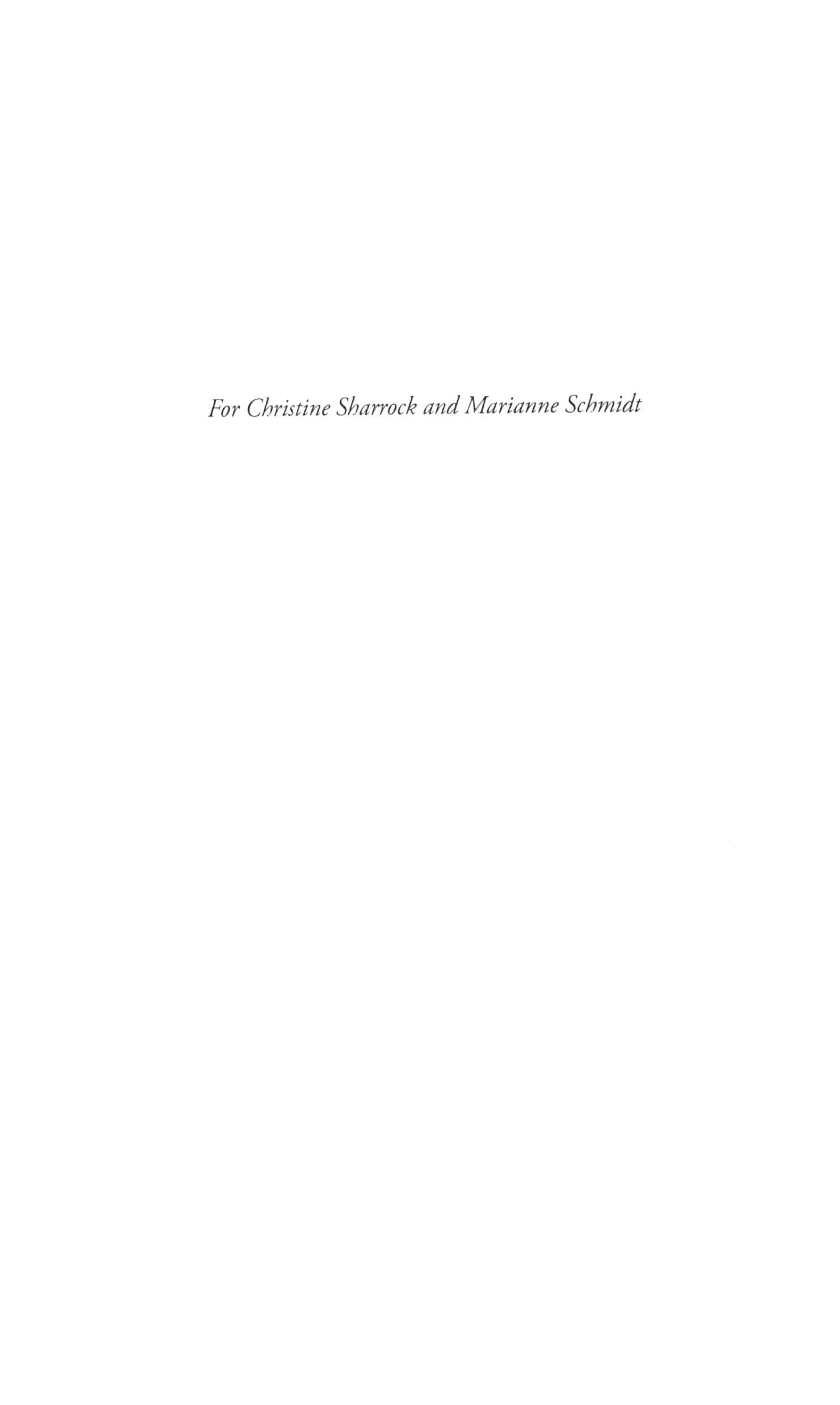

For Christine Sharrock and Marianne Schmidt

ACKNOWLEDGMENTS

My sincere thanks to the people who consented to be interviewed for this book: Rolphe Bandte, John Beer, Detective Senior Constable Stephen Bridge, Dennis Dostine, Barry Ezzy, Detective Inspector Wayne Hayes, Don Jones, Margaret Kavazos, Keith Paull, Steve Raymond, Peter Smith and Detective Sergeant Carla Tomadini.

This book could not have been written without the help of Detective Inspector Russell Oxford. My sincere thanks also to Fiona Schultz and Anouska Good at New Holland Publishers for their support and enthusiasm for this project. Thanks also to Ross Neilson, Keith Smith, Steve Martin, Peter Muhlbock, John McKay, Graeme Fletcher and Fran Dyke, and to Stuart and Mike Smith for their assistance. My sincere thanks also to Claire de Medici for her painstaking work in editing this book.

CONTENTS

PREFACE

On Monday, 11 January 1965, Christine Sharrock and Marianne Schmidt, fifteen-year-old neighbours from the Sydney suburb of West Ryde, travelled by train to Cronulla Beach along with Marianne's three younger brothers and sister. In the early afternoon the two older girls took the Schmidt children for a walk across the sandhills at nearby Wanda Beach. When the wind became too strong for the children, Christine and Marianne left them sheltering behind a dune on the pretext of returning to Cronulla to collect the group's belongings for the train journey home. The children never saw Christine or Marianne alive again.

When the bodies of the two girls were found buried in the sand the following day, one of the largest manhunts in Australian history swung into action. The death of two teenage girls, raped and murdered on a popular Sydney beach, shocked the nation. In the 1960s, a time when the Western world was enjoying an explosion in youth culture, the murders signalled a loss of innocence for the Australian public.

The Wanda Beach murders, as the deaths of Christine Sharrock and Marianne Schmidt became known, remain one of the most infamous unsolved crimes in Australian history. Today, the mere mention of the word 'Wanda' is enough to send a whole generation of baby boomers back to their teenage years — and for the wrong reasons. For them, Wanda Beach will forever be associated with the brutal murder of two teenage girls. It is a crime shrouded in secrecy, myth and misunderstanding, with the countless suspects and theories that have been brought to light over the past thirty-eight years continually fascinating and horrifying us.

The story behind the Wanda Beach murders — and the subsequent police investigation — has never before been told. The primary reason for writing this book was not to sensationalise what was an abominable crime: the facts concerning the deaths of Christine and Marianne speak for themselves. This book needed to be written because the two young girls who lost their lives at Wanda Beach all those years ago were more than simply murder victims; they were just like any other teenagers, with hopes and dreams, and families and friends who loved them and suffered greatly after the girls' deaths.

During the writing of this book, the NSW Police allowed me access to some of the eighty volumes of archived police material involving over 10,000 pages of interviews manually typed on original police running sheets. These files provided a foundation for re-creating events, as well as putting forward police theories that resulted from their investigations (unless otherwise noted). In some chapters, the names of witnesses and suspects have been changed to protect their identity, and these have also been noted in the text. All other names of people who played a major part in the original police investigation remain unchanged, as does material from these original running sheets, including statements and verbatim interviews with witnesses and suspects.

Many of the detectives who originally worked on the investigation have now passed away. For many, such as former Detective Sergeant Cecil Johnson, the Wanda Beach murders remained a haunting influence throughout their lives. Johnson's obsession with one of the Wanda suspects remains an integral part of the mystery that engulfs the case. Former Detective Sergeant Keith Paull, who worked with Johnson and later took charge of the investigation, provided an excellent insight into the case. Paull, who is eighty-two years old and lives in quiet retirement, consented to an interview while remaining extremely conscious of not compromising what remains an open, ongoing investigation. After going through the NSW Police Media Unit, detectives currently investigating Wanda Beach and a number of other unsolved crimes also proved helpful, while taking great pains to maintain the integrity of their current investigations.

While the surviving members of the Schmidt family, including those at the beach the day the girls died, declined to comment — a decision I understand and respect — many friends of the girls and eyewitnesses to their final hours were re-interviewed specifically for this book. Their reminiscences add a new dimension to the clinical statements taken by police in 1965 and in many instances their stories were poignant, heartfelt and, in the case of Margaret Kavazos, Christine Sharrock's childhood friend, somewhat therapeutic.

Christine Sharrock and Marianne Schmidt do not deserve to be remembered merely as victims; footnotes in the annals of Australian criminal history. *Wanda: The Untold Story of the Wanda Beach Murders* is their story and it needs to be told.

Alan J Whiticker

CHAPTER 1
THE LAST DAYS OF INNOCENCE

During that summer, the Daily Telegraph Sand Models Contest encouraged children and teenagers to sculpt models in the sand at local beaches, with weekly winners taking part in a final at Bondi Beach on 30 January.

Looking at a map of the east coast of Australia, one cannot help but notice the narrow corridor of land between the Pacific Ocean and the nondescript group of mountains named the Great Dividing Range — this area is home to the majority of the Australian population. With 36,000 kilometres of coastline, Australia holds any number of beaches, both popular and remote, for people to pursue the Australian dream of sun, sand and surf. It is no wonder the beach is an integral part of Australia's history, culture and myth.

Many writers and social commentators have suggested that the beach has replaced the bush as the mythical home of the modern Australian. The beach is much more accessible to suburban Australia than the traditional bush and has become an essential part of the national identity, producing the bronzed Aussie stereotype and providing a context for other nationalities, especially immigrants, to relate to Australians.

Australian beach culture, especially interest in surfing, exploded in the suburbs in the early 1960s, with ordinary kids catching the wave of enthusiasm, via Hawaii, from America's west coast. Australian teens embraced music by

The Beach Boys, Jan & Dean, and our own Billy Thorpe and the Aztecs, who got their break as the house band at the popular Surf City nightspot in the heart of Kings Cross; they adopted the fashions, spoke the language, and suburban boys dreamt of owning a surfboard. (This was still several years before the women's liberation movement and the common mantra at the time was 'chicks don't surf'.) The dream of riding a surfboard was not limited to those teenagers who lived in seaside suburbs and could see the beach from their front verandah: in Sydney, kids from as far away as the outer western suburbs had that same dream.

During the 1960s Australians Nat Young and 'Midget' Farrelly dominated world surfing championships. The rise in popularity of 'surfies' — tanned, blond (bleached or natural) surfboard riders — brought them into direct confrontation with 'bodgies and widgies' — male and female 'rockers' who were the last remnants of the Elvis-dominated 1950s. This was particularly the case in the beachside suburb of Cronulla, south of Sydney, where any number of stand-offs degenerated into rumbles or brawls between the rival groups on Friday and Saturday nights outside the shops and pubs that lined the main strip into Cronulla.

Bate Bay, immediately south of Botany Bay, is rimmed by Sydney's longest span of beaches; a sweeping arc of sand almost five kilometres long. Four separate beaches — Cronulla, North Cronulla, Elouera and Wanda — are lined together in the bottom half of the bay, with the northernmost section of beach backed by a nature reserve.

The area north of Wanda Beach is known as Greenhills, named after the washed-out, pale-green sand dunes that once ran 3.5 kilometres to Pimelwi Rocks at the northern point of the bay. The area is familiar to Australian audiences, as several classic Australian movies — from *Forty Thousand*

Horsemen in the 1940s, to *Puberty Blues* and *Mad Max III* in the 1980s — as well as countless television commercials were filmed there.

During the Depression there was a cluster of old shacks at nearby Boat Harbour, but the development of the Kurnell Oil Refinery in the 1950s saw any chance of the development of a residential area die out. Over the past thirty years, the sandhills closest to the sea have been both mined out by concrete companies and washed flat by huge seas that hit the bay during the late 1980s and early 1990s. The sand dunes behind the beach are only accessible by four-wheel drive, contrasting with the southern part of the bay that is today a highly developed tourist area.

Despite North Cronulla originally being declared unsafe for bathing by a government committee in 1919, the area grew in popularity and a Surf Lifesaving Club was formed in 1924. The surf lifesaving movement, now an Australian social institution, quickly took hold at Cronulla Beach, because it was the only beach in Sydney serviced by a railway. In an October 2002 interview for this book, Barry Ezzy, a former lifeguard in the local Sutherland Shire during the 1960s, recalled:

> *Not a lot of people had cars in those days … People were a lot more reliant on public transport than they are today. The beach was much more popular then it is today because there's just so much more to do now. In the sixties during summer, the beach was the place to be.*

However, the beach meant different things to different people, as Ezzy described:

> *There was a distinct culture between the surfboard riders and the 'clubbies' … The board riders wanted to*

maintain a separate identity to the members of the surf club. The board riders did their own thing and didn't want to be regimented by the surf club people like me, who were very much involved in the surf lifesaving movement and whose main objective in life was competition in surf lifesaving.

To the true surfer, the beach was a way of life bordering on religious devotion; for the surf lifesaver it became a source of immense pride and competition; and for the ordinary suburban family it was a chance to spend precious leisure hours away from the bustle and grind of daily life. And this was especially true for the millions of immigrants who came to these shores after the end of World War II. The beach seemed to symbolise the best of everything an Australian way of life had to offer.

In the twenty years following 1945 Australia adopted an ambitious reconstruction and expansion program. The realisation that Australia needed a larger population to fulfil this plan — and also to defend itself if invaded — led to the Federal Government's call to 'populate or perish'. In 1945 the Labor Government launched the first Migration Program, which was intended to increase migration to 1 per cent in order to increase the annual population growth rare to 2 per cent.

The following year the government provided assisted passage for British migrants, especially ex-servicemen and their families. This was later expanded to include other countries such as the United States, Italy, Greece, Spain, France, the Netherlands, Norway, Switzerland, Belgium and Denmark. Despite Australia's involvement in two world wars against Germany, German nationals were considered highly desirable migrants in the government's post-war resettlement program. Australia and West Germany reached an agreement in 1952 to assist 3000 Germans per annum, and another 1000 were offered unassisted passage.

Although Australia's population growth rate did not reach the projected 2 per cent per annum, the millionth post-war immigrant arrived on these shores in 1955. The following year Australia modified conditions to make it easier for migrants of non-European descent to gain entry into Australia. In 1956 the Federal Government commenced Operation Reunion, a scheme designed to reunite migrants from (the then) USSR and eastern Europe with relatives who had already settled in Australia. An uprising in Hungary against Communist control also led to Australia accepting 14,000 Hungarian refugees that year. In 1957 the 'Bring out a Briton' campaign encouraged the public to sponsor a British family and assist them in settling in Australia.

In 1958 an important development occurred in the history of Australian migration with the introduction of the *Revised Migration Act*. The new Act abolished the controversial and racially biased dictation test that was compulsory for all prospective migrants. The test was predominantly in English and subsequently, a low percentage of non-English speaking migrants passed. That same year, an agreement of assisted passage with West Germany was renewed. From July 1949 to June 1959, Australia accepted 162,756 German-born immigrants — the third highest number behind the United Kingdom and Italy — representing 13 per cent of all migration during this period. Between 1951 and 1962, 84 per cent of German migrants received assisted passage to Australia.

The Schmidt family was one of the many German families that took up the Australian Government's offer of a new life. Helmut and Elizabeth Schmidt were the parents of six children — Helmut (born 1948), Marianne (born 1949), Hans (born 1952), Peter (born 1954), Trixie (born

1955) and Wolfgang (born 1957) — when they immigrated to Australia. (Elizabeth Schmidt also had a son, Robert Hauschberger, from her first marriage. Robert remained in West Germany and the family lost contact with him in early 1964.) Despite having no family living in Australia, the Schmidt family made the trip and arrived in Melbourne on 13 September 1958 and stayed at the Bonegilla Migrant Camp before moving to the Greta Camp and then Unanderra Migrant Hostel in New South Wales. There they developed friendships with the Bandte, Sterker and Kruger families before moving to the Riverina town of Temora. A seventh child, Norbert, was born to Helmut and Elizabeth in 1959.

On 10 March 1963 the Schmidt family moved to Sydney after securing a housing commission residence in Bush Road, West Ryde. Helmut Schmidt was a carpenter but could not find steady work because of the onset of Hodgkin's disease, a form of cancer that attacks the lymph glands, which ultimately claimed his life on 15 June 1964.

When the Schmidt family moved into their former war service home in West Ryde, Christine Sharrock was living next door with her grandparents, Jim and Jeanette Taig. Christine, who chose to live with her grandparents after her mother remarried and moved to the north-western Sydney suburb of Seven Hills, struck up an immediate friendship with Marianne Schmidt. Although the pair attended different schools, Christine and Marianne both sat for the Leaving Certificate at the end of 1964 and were awaiting their results over the summer holidays.

The Australian public approached the 1965 New Year with great optimism. With a population of eleven million, Australia was basking in the overflow of the economic, political and cultural revolution that had hit other industrialised Western nations. But in many ways,

Australia was still a conservative stronghold. The Federal Liberal Government had been in power since 1949, with leader Robert Menzies in the final twelve months of what would be a record seventeen years as prime minister. On 15 January, swimming sensation Dawn Fraser became the youngest person to be named Australian of the Year, at the not-so-young age of twenty-seven. The news media at the time was also conservative and reactionary. Australia was still getting over the stir caused by the June 1964 tour of The Beatles when The Rolling Stones held their first tour of Australia in January 1965. The fact that a girl's dress was ripped in a 'riot' at Sydney airport was enough to make the front page of at least one newspaper.[1] Australian society was naïve, provincial and insular. During that summer, the *Daily Telegraph* Sand Models Contest encouraged children and teenagers to sculpt models in the sand at local beaches, with weekly winners taking part in a final at Bondi Beach on 30 January. When Merrick Fry, on holiday from Bathurst, won a heat of the competition for his model of a boy scout at North Narrabeen, he was awarded a £3 cash prize, a Streets ice-cream pack and a Supertex beach towel.

In the early hours of Tuesday, 12 January 1965 teenagers waited in Castlereagh Street, Sydney, for the results of the Leaving Certificate published in the early edition newspapers. For years it had been the practice of the major newspapers to publish the examination results in proof form before the newspapers were printed, with teenagers cramming the streets outside the News Ltd offices to check the results. That year, however, the NSW education department requested that the newspapers not publish the results in proof form, ensuring that teenagers would keep a long night's vigil outside newspaper offices until the newspaper hit the streets at around 3 a.m.

At the same time another vigil was being kept, in

adjoining homes in working-class West Ryde. The younger Schmidt children had returned home from their outing to the beach without their sister Marianne and her friend Christine. One part of the Australian dream, Wanda Beach, would soon be forever associated with the brutal murder of two teenage girls.

CHAPTER 2
MONDAY, 11 JANUARY 1965

'It would be fun if we could walk across the sandhills again', Christine said to her grandmother.

'Don't go today, love', Mrs Taig told her. 'You have got the four little ones with you … it's too far.'

'But we would only be away from them for half an hour', Christine argued.

'No, you stay with the children.'

The last conversation Christine Sharrock had with her grandmother before leaving for the beach with Marianne Schmidt and the younger Schmidt children[1]

On the morning of Monday, 11 January 1965 a pall of smoke hung over Sydney. Over the weekend, fire burning in a gully north of Sydney at Narrabeen stretched westward to the Wakehurst Parkway at Mona Vale Road, stopping only when it met the charred ground and burned trees at Terrey Hills that had been damaged in fires some weeks earlier. In the Royal National Park, south of the city, fires burned at Bundeena on an eight-mile front until rain that fell on Sunday had finally quelled them. Strong southerly winds that day would soon blow the smoke away.

Two days earlier, on the afternoon of Saturday, 9 January, Marianne Schmidt and Christine Sharrock had visited Marianne's mother in Sydney's King George V Hospital, where she was recovering from surgery. Mrs Schmidt had left Marianne in charge of her younger siblings, and during the hospital visit Marianne asked if she and Christine could take the children to the beach the following day. Mrs Schmidt understood the beach to be Cronulla, as that was the only beach Marianne had been to. In the last years of his life, Mr Schmidt had taken his family to Cronulla Beach for picnics on the rocks at the southern end of the bay and Cronulla held a special significance for Marianne, who was very close to her father. Only the week before, all seven Schmidt children had travelled to Cronulla Beach for the day.

'Mum, would it be all right if I take sandwiches for all of us and Christine will take the drink?', Marianne asked.

'You can go if you are careful', Mrs Schmidt said to her daughter. 'Watch out for the small ones.' It rained heavily the following day, so the children did not go to the beach. They planned to go the next day — Monday, 11 January.

Early that morning, Marianne Schmidt prepared her four younger siblings — ten-year-old Peter, nine-year-old Trixie, seven-year-old Wolfgang and five-year-old Norbert — for their journey to Cronulla Beach. Two of Marianne's brothers, sixteen-year-old Helmut and thirteen-year-old Hans, stayed behind at their Brush Road home: Helmut to paint the kitchen for his mother while she was in hospital and Hans to mow the lawn. Marianne prepared sandwiches of Marmite (an alternative form of Vegemite), and cucumber and tomato, and packed these with some oranges and apricots and a thermos of cold water in her blue-and-white striped beach bag, along with a red towel.

Next door, Christine Sharrock also made ready for the trip to the beach. She had spent New Year's Day at Cronulla Beach with Marianne, when they had walked across the sandhills at Wanda Beach, but she did not join the Schmidts on their 2 January trip. Christine prepared a thermos of lime-green cordial but did not pack any lunch, telling her 63-year-old grandmother, Jeanette Taig, that she would buy some hot chips for lunch with the £1 note she had been given. (These and other minute details of the trip would later provide important clues to the girls' final movements.)

Christine had a conversation with her nan about her trip to the beach that day and told her:

'It would be fun if we could walk across the sandhills again'.

'Don't go today, love', Mrs Taig told her. 'You have got the four little ones with you … it's too far.'

'But we would only be away from them for half an hour', Christine argued.

'No, you stay with the children.'

Inside her white-and-gold beach bag, Christine packed a red-and-white beach towel, a plastic change purse, a pair of sunglasses and a transistor radio she had received for Christmas. She did not pack a swimming costume or wear one underneath her clothes because she was menstruating at the time and did not intend to swim.

Shortly before 8.30 a.m., Christine and Marianne walked with the younger Schmidt children to the bottom of Brush Road to catch a bus to West Ryde railway station, but when a bus did not come, the group of six walked to the station. After travelling by train to Redfern they changed platforms for the trip to Cronulla, arriving there sometime before 11.00 a.m.

Leaving Cronulla station, Christine, Marianne and the children walked across Cronulla Street and down a lane that led through a small park and past some shops and a fun parlour. They then crossed Gerrale Street, which ran parallel to the beach, and went through Cronulla Park, past the lifesaving club and onto the footpath that led down to the main surfing beach. There they found the beach closed for swimming due to strong southerly winds and treacherous seas, so Christine and Marianne took the children to the southern end of the beach where they sat on some rock shelves.

Wolfgang repeatedly asked to go for a swim, and after a while Marianne took him into the surf where it was shallow and away from the rocks. The group then shared the sandwiches and fruit Marianne had brought, still sitting on the rocks. When they had finished lunch Marianne suggested they walk to the sandhills past Wanda Beach, so the group hid their bags among the rocks and walked along the promenade to North Cronulla Beach. The group moved onto the sand and, in the strong wind, walked past the unpatrolled Elouera Beach to a point 200 yards[2] past the Wanda surf club. At around 1.00 p.m. Christine, Marianne and the children stopped behind a sandhill to shelter from the wind.

With the smaller children complaining about the wind-driven sand hurting their legs, Marianne told them that she and Christine would go back to Cronulla to collect the beach bags they had hidden among the rocks and then return to collect the children and take them home. They left the children crouching out of the wind behind the sandhill, covering them with some of the towels and leaving them Christine's transistor radio for company. Strangely, the two girls then walked off in a northerly direction towards Kurnell, away from where their bags were hidden. When Peter Schmidt called out to the girls that they were going the wrong way, the girls turned and laughed, Christine tripping over in the sand some 150 yards from the water's edge.

This was the last time the Schmidt children saw Christine and Marianne alive.

Peter, Trixie, Wolfgang and Norbert waited in the dunes until 5.00 p.m., building sandcastles and listening to music, before walking back to Cronulla. There, on the rocks at the southern end of the beach, they found their belongings untouched, with the older girls' return train tickets and money purses intact. The children caught the last train out of Cronulla railway station at about 6.00 p.m. and arrived home to West Ryde sometime after 8.00 p.m. At this time Helmut Schmidt was visiting his mother in hospital, and the children informed their brother Hans that the girls had 'gone missing'. Hans took Christine's beach bag into her grandmother's house and informed her that Christine and Marianne had gone for a walk across the sandhills after lunch and had not returned.

During Helmut's visit to his mother at 7.00 p.m., he told her he was worried about his siblings: 'They went to the beach this morning and when I left home at half past five tonight they weren't home'. Before Helmut left his mother at 8.00 p.m., he said he would ring Mrs Taig from nearby Prince Alfred Hospital — a friend of his worked there — and ask if the girls had returned home. Helmut also promised to notify his mother once he confirmed the situation at home, but Mrs Schmidt did not receive a phone call from Helmut that night.

Fears for the girls' safety had not yet overtaken Christine's grandmother when she reported them missing to Ryde police at 8.30 p.m. Her main concern when Constables Newton and Galvin arrived at her home at about 11.40 that night was that the girls would not be able to get home — the other children had brought home the beach bags containing the rail tickets and money and she thought they were probably stranded at Cronulla railway station. When the police visited the Schmidt home, Helmut reiterated the story his brothers and sister had told him that night after he returned home from the hospital, about the girls walking across the sandhills after lunch and not returning.

When the constables asked to speak to the children, Helmut told them he would rather they questioned the children in the morning if necessary, as they were very tired from their day at the beach. He then provided a description and photograph of Marianne. As Galvin took notes, Newton questioned Helmut about whether Marianne and Christine had boyfriends or associated with any boys. Could the girls have run away and were staying with someone they knew?

'No', Helmut said. 'I have never heard any girl mention any boys and the only reason they go to Cronulla is that they can go there by train from West Ryde. They have always gone there.'

When asked how long the girls had been going to Cronulla, Helmut told the police the girls had been there 'quite a few times', but was unable to provide any further information.

What the families and police did not know was that the girls were already dead, buried in the hollow of a sandhill at Wanda Beach. Their bodies would be discovered the following day, sparking the most intensive police investigation ever seen in Australia.

When investigating police endeavoured to piece together the final movements of the two girls, they interviewed Marianne's siblings and questioned those who either came forward with information or were identified as being at Wanda Beach on 11 January 1965. Police used the following eyewitness accounts to fill in the missing gaps and continually form and discount theories about the fate of the two girls.

Although the day was blustery and overcast, there were a number of people at Wanda Beach and in the sandhills area on the afternoon of Monday, 11 January. Dennis Dostine, a

32-year-old fire officer from Sylvania Heights, had taken his six-year-old son for a walk along the beach to Boat Harbour at Kurnell. Dostine knew Wanda Beach well and was a frequent visitor to Wanda Surf Club. When interviewed for this book in October 2002, he recalled: 'The wind was blowing a strong southerly. There had been some big seas prior to the Monday and the beach was rather steep. The dry sand on top of the wet beach was stinging our legs, particularly my son, who was very young at the time.'

On his way back to the Wanda Surf Club in the early afternoon, Dostine noticed two girls on horseback. A pony club was located nearby and the sandhills were a popular place for horseriding. Later he noticed a different pair of girls riding horses. At about 12.45 p.m. Dostine passed a male youth walking along the water's edge: he described the man as approximately nineteen years old, tall, with light-coloured hair and a noticeably pale complexion. The youth was dressed in khaki cotton shorts and a white nylon short-sleeved shirt. It was estimated that Dostine passed this youth about 400 yards north of the murder scene, near a local land feature called the 'Big Hill'.

Dostine kept walking towards Wanda and at a point 800 yards north of the surf club saw two teenage girls walking in a northerly direction along the sandhills. He watched the girls for barely a minute as they hurried northward in a 'fast walk' across a level expanse of sand about 200 yards from the water's edge. During his 1965 interview with police he noted:

> *We were almost back at the Wanda Surf Club when I noticed the two girls going in the opposite direction with the wind blowing at their backs … One of the girls was looking back over her shoulder as if she was expecting to be followed. I probably thought at the time how much the sand would have been stinging their legs.*

Although he was not close enough to positively identify Christine and Marianne, Dostine's general description matched the girls' appearance that day. Dostine described the girls as in their early teens and of slight build. One was wearing a blue–green blouse, the other what appeared to be black stretch shorts. Although Dostine noticed that one of the girls was frequently looking back over her shoulder, he did not see anyone following them.

As the wind was at their backs, they could have been looking behind them because they expected to be followed by one of the younger children, or because they had noticed a stranger following them.

Dostine lost sight of the girls when they walked behind some sandhills; he estimated the time to be about 1.00 p.m. because he arrived at Wanda Surf Club at 1.05 p.m. While walking with his son, Dostine also observed a man and a woman 'play fighting' on the beach, some couples sunbaking on the sand and a group of young boys and girls fossicking around in the sandhills. Shortly before he arrived at the club, he passed another man walking in a northerly direction along the water's edge. This man was 40–50 years old, 5 feet 5 inches tall with a strong, stocky build. The man was well tanned and wore a pair of old black cotton trunks and carried a beach towel. As the man passed, he casually said to Dostine, 'It's a windy day'.

'Yes, it is', Dostine replied and then walked up towards the surf club. During his interview for this book, Dostine recalled that the day the bodies were discovered, he was visiting his mother-in-law in the suburb of Kogarah when the news came over the radio that two bodies had been discovered in the sand at Wanda Beach and that the police were appealing to anyone who had any information to come forward:

> *It was just too much of a coincidence, rather strange in fact, that I had passed two girls on the beach the previous day … so I rang Kogarah police station. A detective came straight over and interviewed me then and there. Later, I went to Cronulla police station, where they took a more detailed account of what I had to say.*

A month later, on 16 February, Dostine accompanied detectives to the area where he had last seen the two girls. The 'flat expanse of ground' the girls were walking on at the time Dostine saw them was 600 yards north of the Wanda Surf Club and in a direct line measuring 400 yards from where the Schmidt children were left sheltering behind a sandhill. Retracing Dostine's steps, starting at a point where he had seen the pale youth, detectives found that it took eight minutes walking southwards to reach the murder scene. It then took a further nine minutes to reach the place where Dostine saw the two girls hurrying across the sand.

Had the pale youth doubled back after passing Dostine and, having encountered the two girls walking northward, murdered them? The timeframe established by investigating detectives made it possible.

When discussing the case during an interview for this book, Dostine noted that he was not impressed when one of the detectives pointed out that he was probably the last person to see the girls alive. 'I took exception to that', he says. He pointed out that the last person to see the girls was the murderer, and Dostine was quickly cleared as a suspect. The two men Dostine described — the tall, pale youth and the 'leathery, suntanned old bloke' — were never identified.

'I couldn't have seen the girls for more than ten to fifteen seconds and hardly noticed them at all when they drew level to me', Dostine remembered. 'Even then, they were about 100 yards away. I really had very little to contribute to the investigation, and the matter has been filed away in the back of my mind for all these years.' No one had spoken to him about the case since 1965.

Dostine was the last person known to police who had seen the girls alive, at around 1.00 p.m. that day. The following accounts were taken from people who were on the beach from this time onwards and could have, during their ordinary day at the beach, been in the vicinity of the murder scene as the girls were being killed and buried.

Louise Coffey and Juleen Williams, from nearby Miranda and roughly the same age as Christine and Marianne, took their horses onto Wanda Beach that day. They, along with Louise's five-year-old brother, were riding near the water's edge when, at about 12.45 p.m., two small boys about nine years old ran up to them and asked to ride the horses.

'You can't have a ride, the horse is too frisky', Louise said. One of the boys took a stick from the sand and shook it at the horse. 'If you don't get away, I'll chase you', Juleen said. The boys ran away, one into the sandhills and the other back towards Wanda Surf Club; Juleen chased them for a few yards before riding off. When the police brought the Schmidt family back to the beach on 26 January, Juleen identified the boys they had chased as Peter and Wolfgang.

After encountering the Schmidt boys, Louise and Juleen continued on horseback in a northerly direction. They saw two or three boys, aged between fourteen and sixteen, accompanied by a dog, playing in the hills about 150 yards north of the Wanda Surf Club. They also saw three other boys running up and down the sandhills some distance from the water's edge but could not provide a description of them. As the girls continued on their way to Boat Harbour, and before they reached Greenhills, they noticed a man standing on the edge of a sandhill. They described him as about thirty years old, 5 feet 9 inches tall, with a stocky build, round face, dark brown hair with a curl on the forehead, and wearing fawn shorts and a bright-coloured shirt.

When the girls arrived at Boat Harbour they began inspecting an old tin shack; as they were doing so their horses galloped off. Leaving Louise's five-year-old brother at the shack, the two girls ran after the horses and followed them up a track where two men from the refinery had captured them. The girls returned to the shack and picked up the young child before beginning their return journey to Wanda at about 3.00 p.m. The dark-haired man was still standing on the sandhill near Greenhills, observing those walking along the water's edge. When Juleen looked back a second time, the man had gone.

At about 3.20 p.m. the two girls on horseback passed a man walking along the water's edge with a white dog on a chain. Further along towards Wanda at about 3.40 p.m. they saw four males in the sandhills. Juleen remarked that the men looked like 'rockers' and that they should stay away from them. Five minutes later, 400 yards south of the murder scene and 800 yards north of the surf club, they saw a man standing in the sandhills wearing long grey baggy trousers and holding a towel that was folded into a bundle. Louise and Juleen did not observe anyone else on the beach that afternoon.

The other pair of horseriders, Jeanine Leyson and Judy Balkwell, were slightly younger than Christine Sharrock and Marianne Schmidt, and did not see the victims or the younger Schmidt children on the beach that day. But had they seen the girls' murderer?

Jeanine and Judy left their Kirawee homes at about 9.45 that morning, arriving at North Cronulla Beach 1–2 hours later and riding along the water's edge towards Boat Harbour. Roughly halfway between North Cronulla Beach and the Big Hill they passed a man rod-fishing on the beach. About half a mile further they saw a man jogging; he was approximately thirty years old with a sturdy build and dark hair and was wearing leopard-print swimming trunks and carrying a towel.

Between 12.45 and 1.15 p.m. — roughly the time Christine and Marianne left the Schmidt children in the sandhills and started their own northerly trek — the two riders rested their horses at the Big Hill landmark, 400 yards north of the eventual murder scene. While resting there, the girls were startled by a naked man who walked out from behind a sandhill about 20 yards to the south of where they were sitting. They described the man as 30–45 years old, medium height, medium-to-heavy build, with dark hair. He was walking south towards Wanda Beach, carrying a bundle of clothes.

Jeanine called out to the man, 'Hey, what are you doing?'. The man looked back over his shoulder and appeared to say something, but the wind was blowing strongly and his words were inaudible. He then continued walking towards Wanda Beach. This man was never identified. The girls returned to Wanda Surf Club, riding in behind the first row of sandhills to protect themselves from the wind. About three-quarters of a mile south of the murder scene, they saw a man and two boys collecting shells. Closer to the surf club, they saw a group of about ten young boys and girls they described as 'surfies', before riding up to the little street at the beachfront at Wanda at about 1.30 p.m. There they ate a hamburger at a local shop before returning home.

Possibly the first sighting of the Schmidt children at Wanda Beach on 11 January was reported by Frank Williams, a 57-year-old Cronulla man who was walking along the beach near the Wanda Surf Club sheds at about midday. Williams saw a man lying in a sand dune near an old demolished house, 50 yards north of the surf club. The man had what appeared to be a piece of corrugated iron, about 12 square inches, over his face. Williams passed within six feet of the man but the sides of the 'corrugated iron' were bent, concealing his head and face. The man was wearing faded blue jeans pulled up to the knees, exposing feet Williams described as 'dirty, big and rough'.

When Williams walked back towards the Wanda Surf Club, he saw six children hurrying along the beach in a northerly direction. The group consisted of two girls, three boys and 'a smaller child'. One of the older girls was wearing a 'floral jacket', while another held the hand of the younger child. One of the boys was running ahead of the group and then running back to join them. Williams later identified the children as the Schmidt children. When Williams passed in front of the Wanda Surf Club he noticed the time was 12.45 p.m. on the surf club clock; he also noted that there were two rod-fishermen at Wanda Beach at the time, about 100 yards apart from each other.

The rod-fishermen were later identified but despite appeals in the Sydney newspapers, the person the press labelled the 'man in the iron mask' was never identified.

John Dickson, a 62-year-old builder from St Peters, was also at Wanda Beach on 11 January. Dickson had been in the habit each Monday of catching a train to Cronulla and walking along the beach to Kurnell for exercise. As he walked along the water's edge on his way to Kurnell he saw two girls come out of the sand dunes. This sighting was a little later than other accounts, walking past the Wanda Surf Club as he did at 2.30 p.m. 'I think that at least one of the girls was in a bathing costume and I am not positive what the other was wearing', he told detectives later that week. 'Both had bare legs and I think that she may have perhaps been wearing shorts.'

It is uncertain whether the two girls Dickson saw were Christine and Marianne. When asked to clarify what age he would estimate the 'young girls' he saw to be, Dickson replied:

> *I am sure they had fairly young faces … I thought that one looked a bit darker than the other. They would be about the same height. When they both came out of the sand dunes one of the girls had her arm around the other.* The problem with this statement was that it was taken on Friday, 15 January, at the end of a week of blanket media coverage. The description of the girls had already been printed in the newspapers, as had a picture of the two girls standing outside their Brush Road homes (one with her arm around the other), and there was a chance Dickson was subconsciously filling in gaps with details he had read.

Dickson also noticed two young men walk out of the sandhills and approach the girls. (Detectives had descriptions of a number of suspects, but the possibility of two murderers could not be discounted.) 'I walked along some distance further and I looked back to see how the weather was and then I noticed that the men were sitting near the girls.' Dickson described the first man as approximately twenty years old, 5 feet 7 inches tall, a well-built, dark-haired, 'clean-cut' man wearing black swimming trunks; the second man was slimmer, also about twenty years old, 5 feet 7–9 inches tall, fair-haired wearing 'some kind of [swimming] costume'. About two thirds of the way around to Kurnell, Dickson passed two girls on horseback (Louise Coffey and Juleen Williams) heading back towards Wanda Beach. On his return journey, when Dickson passed the point where he had seen the unidentified girls and the two men, there was no sign of anyone. At this time the weather was very inclement, with wind blowing sand around in 'fairly strong gusts'. Dickson walked back to Cronulla railway station and caught a 5.15 p.m. train home.

Of the many eyewitness accounts taken by police from people at Wanda Beach on the day of the murders, Dennis Dostine's established the last official sighting of Christine and Marianne — shortly before 1.00 p.m. and heading in a northerly direction towards Kurnell. However, the failure to identify the 'pale youth' and 'leathery old man' left detectives little to work with. Similarly, the failure to identify the 'man in the iron mask' — or at least explain what he was doing — left another hole in the investigation. The evidence supplied by the two pairs of young horseriders corroborated Dostine's information but did not lead to the identification of any other suspect.

The day the girls' bodies were found, Wolfgang Schmidt revealed to police that he had seen a blond-haired youth walking with Christine and Marianne into the sandhills. Despite the accounts of other eyewitnesses at Wanda Beach on 11 January, this 'blond-haired surfie' described by Wolfgang became the prime suspect. Early in the investigation, detectives formed the opinion that the girls could have known their killer and arranged to meet him in the sandhills, and police focused much time and attention on trying to prove this theory.

CHAPTER 3
CHRISTINE AND MARIANNE

Sunday, 3 January 1965

Rolf came up this afternoon. He didn't even talk [to] me. I had a good old cry. I hope I never see him again.

Christine Sharrock's final diary entry prior to her death

Friday, 8 January 1965

Happy birthday Elvis. I think I love Elvis. Not for his money but himself. Heard Elvis's songs all day. Helmut & Hans visited Mum (in hospital). Did the washing and ironing.

Marianne Schmidt's final diary entry prior to her death

Who were Christine Sharrock and Marianne Schmidt? While many Australians became familiar with the facts surrounding their deaths, no one outside the tight-knit circle of family and friends really knew the girls. They were more than simply murder victims to be dissected by the media and consumed by the public; Christine and Marianne had plans, goals, insecurities and problems like any other teenager.

Marianne Schmidt was born on 30 October 1949 in Hof, Bavaria, in West Germany, and was eight years old when her family migrated to Australia. After the death of Marianne's father in 1964, the Schmidt family eked out a simple existence, living on Mrs Schmidt's widow pension while Marianne's older brother, Helmut, worked as an apprentice electrician for the NSW Government Railways. Every second Sunday, the

Schmidt children travelled to Rookwood Cemetery with their mother and placed flowers on their father's grave.

When Marianne was ten years old, she confided in her mother that she wanted to be an airline hostess. Her mother, however, always told her that she would never be able to afford this and encouraged Marianne to 'think about getting a boyfriend and when she was old enough, getting married'. Marianne attended Marsden High School in Winbourne Street, Ermington, situated on a hill that overlooked the Schmidt's modest brick house in Brush Road, West Ryde. She completed her third year of high school in 1964 and intended to continue her studies into Form Four (Year 10) and obtain her Intermediate Certificate at the end of 1965. Marianne's mother wanted her to complete a secretarial course when she left school and Marianne had won a scholarship to a nearby technical college. Mrs Schmidt planned to discuss her daughter's options with the headmaster of Marsden High School when school resumed in late January 1965. One of these options included Marianne receiving private tuition in Spanish and Italian so she could master these languages; she had gained 98 per cent in German, 76 per cent in French and well over 80 per cent in English, and wanted to see Europe again before considering marriage.

Mrs Schmidt described Marianne as a well-behaved girl who 'did her homework regularly'. She rarely went out socially, except to take her brothers and sister to nearby Ryde swimming pool or to go next door to talk to her friend, Christine Sharrock. Marianne rarely attended picture shows or dances, her mother maintained; she spent all her time at home and playing with the children.

When asked about boys Christine and Marianne associated with, Mrs Schmidt said that although Marianne had told her she 'liked the faces of certain boys at school', she 'did not have a boyfriend that she was in love with', and

Mrs Schmidt did not know if Christine had a boyfriend.

When the Schmidt family arrived in Brush Road in 1963, Christine Sharrock was living there with her grandparents, Jim and Jeanette Taig. Christine and Marianne immediately struck up a friendship. When police visited Mrs Taig on the night of the girls' disappearance on 11 January 1965, she told them the two girls were 'inseparable' and 'always in each other's homes'. Christine would often go next door at night, usually to watch television or to talk with Marianne or help her with her chores; Christine always had to be home by 9.00 p.m. The closeness in the girls' ages — their birthdays were just twenty-five days apart — meant that the girls shared many interests including clothes, music and a natural interest in boys. The girls were even similar in appearance: both were about five feet tall, although Marianne was slightly taller at 5 feet 2 inches, and both had naturally curly hair (although Christine had always tried to straighten hers) — Marianne's was dark while Christine's was golden brown.

There was also the special bond of both girls having lost fathers they adored. Christine, who was born on 5 October 1949, came from a loving but troubled family. Her mother, Beryl, had remarried and lived 15 kilometres away in Seven Hills with her second husband, Barry Maher, and their son, Graham. Christine did not feel part of her new step-family and stayed with a succession of friends and relatives before moving in with her grandparents.

When interviewed for this book in November 2002, Margaret Kavazos, Christine's childhood friend from St Therese's Catholic Girls' School at Lakemba, described the situation:

Christine was rebellious in her own way and I don't think her mother had the energy to fight her ... Mrs Maher was grief-stricken ... following the death of her

> *first husband. She had made a new life for herself with her [new] husband and young son. I know it sounds terrible but Christine never wanted to be with her family … she was very strong-minded. She used to say that she didn't like her step-dad, who was a very good man, but she never really got over the death of her father. She was happiest living with her nan at West Ryde.*

Despite living in West Ryde, Christine returned to St Therese's at Lakemba after several years at another school to maintain contact with her old school friends again, especially Margaret. Christine caught the bus from Victoria Road to Ryde railway station every morning, making the train trip to Lakemba and then back again — a trip that added over an hour of travel to her day. Christine and Margaret completed Third Form (Year 9) in 1964. 'It was the first year of the Wyndham Scheme', Margaret says. 'We had the choice to sit the Leaving Certificate in Year 9 or to go on and do the Higher School Certificate.' Christine finished school in December and three weeks before Christmas obtained a job in the stationery section at Anthony Horden's department store in West Ryde.

Although living with her grandparents provided a strict, conservative upbringing, Christine was becoming more independent. She had only been to Cronulla Beach once prior to the day of her death, and had not even owned a swimming costume until shortly before (she had borrowed one from Marianne on previous occasions). While working at Anthony Horden's during the summer Christine had struck up a friendship with nineteen-year-old salesgirl Lafayre Miller, and had even gone to a drivein movie with Lafayre and her boyfriend. Christine had also developed a friendship with Neil Macken, a Year 11 student at Marsden High School who also worked at Anthony Horden's. On several occasions, Neil had walked Christine home to Brush Road, and she had invited him to attend a party with her in Beverley Hills on the weekend of 16 January but had to introduce him to her nan first. As Neil drove to work on Monday, 11 January 1965, he passed Christine, Marianne and the Schmidt children as they walked towards the railway station on their way to Cronulla Beach.

The following diary entries from Christine and Marianne reveal the suburban hopes and aspirations of two normal fifteen-year-old girls and provide a poignant insight into the ordinary lives of the two deceased girls.[1]

Marianne Schmidt:

Tuesday, 1 December 1964
Summer started today, read Chris my diary. Gang's attitude has changed. Robert was at school today — boy. Nearly pushed Tony down the stairs — wish I had. Robert went home at lunchtime.

Wednesday, 2 December 1964
Norbert's birthday today. Curled Christine's hair for [her] first day of work. Boy — do I wish Robert really likes me. Made up my mind to get heart (locket) engraved 'Rob'.

Thursday, 3 December 1964
When I went shopping I saw Greg and Barry. Christine's first day of work, she liked it. I decided to work at A.H.'s [Anthony Horden's] on Saturdays. Nothing exciting happened. (*All next year.)*

Friday, 4 December 1964
Robert stayed home, so did Anna and Liz. Had to hand

our textbooks in today. Rolf's coming tomorrow. I like Tony but I love Rob. I wish he'd do something decisive.

Saturday, 5 December 1964
Went to see 'Come Blow Your Horn' with Frank Sinatra. Roy stayed at Kruger's place. Kim (Leferre's [sic] sister) goes to M.H.S. [Marsden High School]

Sunday, 6 December 1964
Was confirmed. Rolf walked with Trudy. Chris is miserable. Quarrelled with Heinz. But I don't care any more. Today cut off [sic] anything between him and me. I like Rolf a lot more.

Friday, 1 January 1965
Was up until 2.30 a.m. Chris came over. Went to the beach today. Met Ted (1), and Jim (2*) today. They kissed us for New Year. Rolf didn't come down today. (1*Chris met him at a school dance.) (2*Don't know his real name.)*

Saturday, 2 January 1965
Could hardly sleep because I went to the beach again and got a [sic] sunburn. Had lots of fun with the boys there. Met Susan [there]. Manfred came down.

Sunday, 3 January 1965
Went for a walk (afternoon) — followed by several boys. Christine doesn't want to see Rolf ever again. Reason — didn't say hallo or goodbye to her. Met George today. (Rolf came down. Mr Bandte signed my autograph book.)

Monday, 4 January 1965

Chris and I disputed our rights and wrongs. I like Rolf now. Chris said she doesn't like him anymore.

Tuesday, 5 January 1965
I took Mum to Hospital. Helmut was stupid enough not to make lunch for the kids. Was nervous. Chris complained about me asking her how mum would be.

Wednesday, 6 January 1965
Took down Christmas decorations. Visited Mum tonight. She was 'fit as [a] fiddle'. Met Miss Evans and Toni again.

Thursday, 7 January 1965
Mum was operated [on] today. I visited her again. She was all right thank goodness. Trudy came down. Spent 3 pounds 11/8 on groceries, 18/6 meat, 10/9 delicatessen.

Friday, 8 January 1965
Happy birthday Elvis. I think I love Elvis. Not for his money but himself. Heard Elvis's songs all day. Helmut & Hans visited Mum (in hospital). Did the washing and ironing.

Christine Sharrock:

Monday, 21 December 1964
I found out Greg likes another girl in cosmetics.

Tuesday, 22 December 1964
I asked Neale [sic] to a party. I have to take him the details tomorrow.

Wednesday, 23 December 1964

He can't go because it is on a Sunday. I had to ring Anne & tell her tomorrow. I also finished work today.

Thursday, 24 December 1964
I rang Anne & and it is on the 16th. Jan. & Neale [sic] is going. I went to midnight mass. Marianne stopped her mother from going.

Saturday, 26 December 1964
Neule [sic] was supposed to come and meet Nan today but he didn't. I think he went yachting.

Tuesday 29 December 1964
I saw Neale [sic] he went to Sutherland & then to Cabarita, that's why he didn't come on Saturday.

Thursday, 31 December 1964
Today is New Years Eve. I saw the New Year through but I cried because Rolf did not come and I was unhappy.

Friday, 1 January 1965
Marianne and I went to Cronulla & we met 2 boys. When they were going they kissed us for New Year.

Saturday, 2 January 1965
Neale [sic] came around and met Nan & she likes him. Thank heavens.

Sunday, 3 January 1965
Rolf came up this afternoon. He didn't even talk [to] me. I had a good old cry. I hope I never see him again.

After the girls' bodies were discovered at Wanda Beach on 12 January 1965 detectives interviewed the people mentioned in the diaries, working on the theory that the girls may have known their killer/s or even arranged to meet him/them at the beach.

The 'Rolf' referred to in both girls' diaries was Rolph Bandte, the sixteen-year-old son of a family the Schmidts befriended at Unanderra Migrant Hostel when they first came to Australia in 1958. When interviewed for this book in November 2002, Rolph recalled:

> *Our families would often visit each other … The adult members of our families became very good friends but I was the same age as Marianne. When the Schmidts moved to Sydney, we used to visit them after Mr Schmidt died and I also got to know Christine, Marianne's next-door neighbour. The girls were happy, fun-loving girls … very friendly. Helmut and myself and the two girls used to go bowling and to the movies. It wasn't like a girlfriend/ boyfriend type of thing, just a group of teenagers enjoying themselves.*

Rolph was unaware that he had played such an important role in the girls' diaries:

> *I was very surprised when the police told me that my name kept appearing in the two girls' diaries … I was a late developer and didn't show that much interest in girls at that stage and I wasn't aware that the girls were even interested. I had known Marianne for years and did not know that her feelings may have changed in any way towards me. Marianne was a very sensible girl with a great sense of humour. We were always laughing and joking together when we visited. Christine was very quiet, not as open as the Schmidt children.*

At the time of the murders, the Bandte family lived in the beachside suburb of Corrimal in Wollongong, south of Sydney. A local sergeant from the Wollongong police interviewed Rolph, not only to eliminate him as a suspect but also to ask him about any other known associates of the girls. Rolph stated that he was at home with his younger brother on the day the girls were murdered and had never even been to the beach before, and in his recent interview commented:

> *Because both girls mentioned me in their diaries, the police came and interviewed me … I wasn't worried about them questioning me because I wanted to help in any way I could but I remember my mother got very angry with the police because they intimated that I could have stolen a car or something and driven up there and done the crime.*

Mrs Bandte told police she had visited Mrs Schmidt in hospital on Thursday, 7 January 1965 and Mrs Schmidt had informed her that Christine carried a picture of Rolph in a locket around her neck and was obviously very fond of him. The deaths of Christine and Marianne hit Rolph hard:

> *We used to get very upset when the police released different details of the crimes, or a new theory about what happened to the girls … When Marianne and Christine were murdered I couldn't believe it. I sat down and cried. You read about things like this but you never believed they could happen to people you knew.*

Although Rolph often caught up with the elder Schmidt boys, the Bandte family gradually lost contact with the Schmidt family over the course of several decades.

The 'Susan' referred to by Marianne in her 2 January entry turned out to be a fellow student from Marsden High School, but she could not add anything of substance to the police investigation. On three occasions that day (2 January), Marianne had walked past the girl and said hello but the two did not have a conversation. Later that afternoon, Susan saw Marianne and her brothers catching the train from Cronulla railway station but did not see Marianne in the company of any other person.

In order to move the investigation forward, police leaked to the media the fact that they wanted to contact the boys — 'Ted and Jim' — who Christine and Marianne had met at Cronulla Beach on New Year's Day. The two boys were later identified as Ted Mylnarz and John Beer, two students from De La Salle College in Marrickville. They were interviewed by Detective Sergeants Keith Paull and Fred Shaw and stated that they had visited Cronulla Beach on 1 January 1965 and met the girls while walking south along the rocks at Cronulla.

John Beer lived in the southwestern Sydney suburb of Greenacre at that time and used to go to Cronulla Beach frequently with a group of school friends. When interviewed for this book in October 2002, Beer remembered:

Cronulla Beach was the 'in' place to go … We never classified ourselves as 'surfies', though. We were just teenagers having a good time. We were on the beach on New Year's Day 1965, when Ted started talking to two girls. Just small talk … 'g'day, nice day, how ya going' … there was nothing unusual about them, just ordinary girls … they were very innocent times and the girls were beyond reproach.

According to Beer's 1965 statement to the police, he and Ted sat on the rocks for two hours, talking with the girls about music, records, school … the usual things teenagers talk about. Both boys stated that the girls conducted themselves 'very well and spoke well'. When the boys left the beach to be picked up by car, the girls walked with them for about 400 yards up to some shops. Christine and Marianne's diaries stated that the boys kissed the girls to celebrate the new year shortly before leaving the beach, although John Beer (when interviewed in 2002) did not remember kissing the girls at any time:

> *I didn't realise it was those girls who had been murdered until the police contacted me … I believe that the police actually took Ted in and questioned [him] because he had blond hair at the time and fit the description of the suspect. They only talked to me at home. We were both terribly shocked. The girls struck us as normal, down-to-earth types.*

The boys did not make arrangements to meet the girls again and did not return to Cronulla Beach between 1 January and the day Christine and Marianne were murdered. Both boys were at work on 11 January and were quickly eliminated as suspects.

In the police copy of Marianne Schmidt's diary, the 5 December reference to 'Kruger' was underlined in red pen by an unknown hand; most likely an investigating detective. The Kruger family lived in Cabramatta and had remained in contact with the Bandte and Schmidt families after meeting them in Wollongong. This reference was to have a sinister, but entirely coincidental, overtone twelve months later.

The bodies of Christine and Marianne were released on Tuesday, 19 January for burial the following day.[2] It was originally reported that the girls' families would conduct a joint service but this did not prove to be the case. The service for Marianne Schmidt was held in the West Chapel of the Metropolitan Funeral Home in Burwood at 11.00 a.m. Elizabeth Schmidt, her face washed of expression after a week of grief and exhaustion, leaned on the arm of her eldest son, Helmut.

Police observed the congregation of mourners, looking for anyone who might fit Wolfgang Schmidt's description of the blond-haired youth he claimed to have seen with his sister and Christine before they died. At that time this youth was considered the most likely suspect and police were working on the assumption that the girls knew their killer; if the youth was an acquaintance of theirs, there was a chance he may attend their funerals. Later, at Rookwood Crematorium, police took photographs of the congregation of mourners for future reference.

Reverends Paesch and Noske, associate ministers of St Paul's Lutheran Church in Sydney, conducted the 50-minute service in which Reverend Noske at times addressed the congregation in the Schmidts' native German:

> *She gave joy to many as a modest, Christian woman. You had high hopes for her … she had bright hopes for a happy future, but by a brutal and bestial act, this has changed … I say to you, Elizabeth, and to the children; comfort each other with thy words … it is well with the child. It is well, indeed today, with Marianne. Believe it my friends; believe it with all your hearts, you will see her again.*

Keith Paull, one of the many detectives who worked on the Wanda case, was interviewed for this book in September 2002 and recalled the day of the girls' funerals:

> *Mrs Schmidt and her children stood up to it all very well — it was obvious that the Schmidt family had a very strong faith in something because they didn't go to pieces. I've seen many relatives and parents of murdered children react differently. A lot of other mothers would not have acted in such a staunch way.*

Prior to the service, detectives interviewed a man and his twin daughters at the West Chapel. The man, George Sterker, had contacted the police to inform them that his daughters had been friends with Marianne and may have information relevant to the investigation. The Sterkers — one of the German families that had befriended the Schmidt family while staying at the Unanderra Migrant Hostel — had recently returned from a holiday in Brisbane and only just learned of the girls' murders. Marianne had recently written to her friends, and Mr Sterker thought they might have information that could help the investigation — a new boyfriend … the name of someone she was perhaps planning to meet at Wanda … anything. The girls were interviewed separately in rooms adjoining the main office but could not provide any clues.

After the funeral service, a cortege of twenty-two cars wound its way to Rookwood Crematorium, where Marianne's body was cremated.

Across town the same day, 200 people gathered at St Michael's Catholic Church in Meadowbank for the funeral of Christine Sharrock. Christine's mother, Beryl Maher (formerly Beryl Sharrock), arrived — a picture of grief — with her husband. Christine's grandfather, James Taig, assisted his wife, Jeanette — 'Nan' to Christine — into the service. Reverend Father Bush, a family friend, and Reverend Father RJ Davey, Liverpool Parish Priest, presided over the service, asking mourners inside the church to also pray for the killer.

After the service, Christine's grandmother collapsed and was placed across the back seat of the mourning coach. A wreath from the Taig family was placed on Christine's coffin; the inscription read, 'With Love, Memories and Thoughts from Four Loved Ones'. Christine's body was later taken to the Catholic section of Liverpool Cemetery, where she was buried beside her father in a family grave. Again, police were on hand to scan mourners for youths fitting the description of the suspect, and photographed all males in attendance at the gravesite.

On 3 and 4 February that year, detectives interviewed the headmasters of Marsden High School, Meadowbank High School and Ryde High School, briefing them on the facts of the case, with a view to addressing all students. The briefing was a harrowing experience for Mr Hagan, the headmaster of Marsden High School, as his principal's residence was in Brush Road, making him a neighbour of the deceased girls. Mr Hagan was reluctant to allow the police to address his pupils and opted to address his students himself. The police wanted the following information:

- the names of students who visited Wanda Beach on 11 January 1965;
- any information concerning males the two girls may have associated with at the beach;
- the names of any males answering the description of the suspect;
- the names of any males closely associated with the deceased; and
- the names of any pupils who had been approached by strangers in the Cronulla–Wanda Beach area.

School friends mentioned in the girls' diaries were routinely interviewed. Each said effectively the same thing: Marianne and Christine were decent, shy girls who did not seem to have any interest in boys outside normal school activities. Many of the students seemed surprised that their names were in the girls' diaries, as they only associated with them casually at school. Police interviews determined that the school friends of Christine and Marianne were not aware of anyone who attended Wanda Beach, carried a knife or had a fascination with the girls.

The murders had at this stage caused a media frenzy, and the parents of some Marsden High School students contacted police with their suspicions of boys with blond hair or those who allegedly owned knives. Two boys from the school were even detained while on holiday in Queensland on the basis that they had blond hair and had gone to school with Marianne Schmidt in 1963, but were quickly eliminated from the inquiry. Two boys from Ryde High School came forward and said they were at Wanda Beach with their parents on 11 January 1965, while a girl from East Hills High School offered the fact that she was a frequent visitor to North Cronulla but had never met Christine and Marianne.

Inquiries were also made at Christine's school — St Therese's Catholic Girls' School in Lakemba — when classes resumed in February. Sister Raymond, the school principal, stated that Christine Sharrock was well known to her and was 'a sensible and well-behaved girl'. Two students who attended Cronulla Beach on the day before the girls were killed and on the day the bodies were found were questioned regarding 'likely suspects or perverts in the Cronulla district or any other likely information', but it came to nought.

By the end of February, police had exhausted the theory that the girls knew their killer; it is plain that this theory had been flawed from the beginning. The girls originally intended to go to the beach on Sunday, 10 January, but changed their plans to the following day because of the poor weather — the likelihood that someone they met at the beach on New Year's Day (or someone Marianne had met while there with her siblings on 2 January) had laid in wait for them to return for the next nine days, seems remote.

But the alternative — that Christine and Marianne were murdered in a random act of violence — was too horrible to contemplate. It made the task of finding the perpetrator almost impossible. There were no eyewitnesses to the crime and very little physical evidence to even link a 'person unknown' to the murder.

Above: Close friends Christine Sharrock (left) and Marianne Schmidt (right) were 'inseparable'. Both were fifteen years old when they were murdered at Wanda Beach on 11 January 1965.

Right: Christine Sharrock as a fourteen-year-old schoolgirl.

Below: Marianne Schmidt in the backyard of her home in West Ryde.

Above: Christine and Marianne lived in these modest ex-serviceman's homes in Brush Road, West Ryde. Christine lived with her grandparents in the house on the left; the Schmidt residence is on the right, *c. 1965.*

Above: The isolated, windswept Greenhills area where the girls' bodies were found. The Kurnell Oil Refinery can be seen in the background. Photographed by investigating police *c. 1965.*

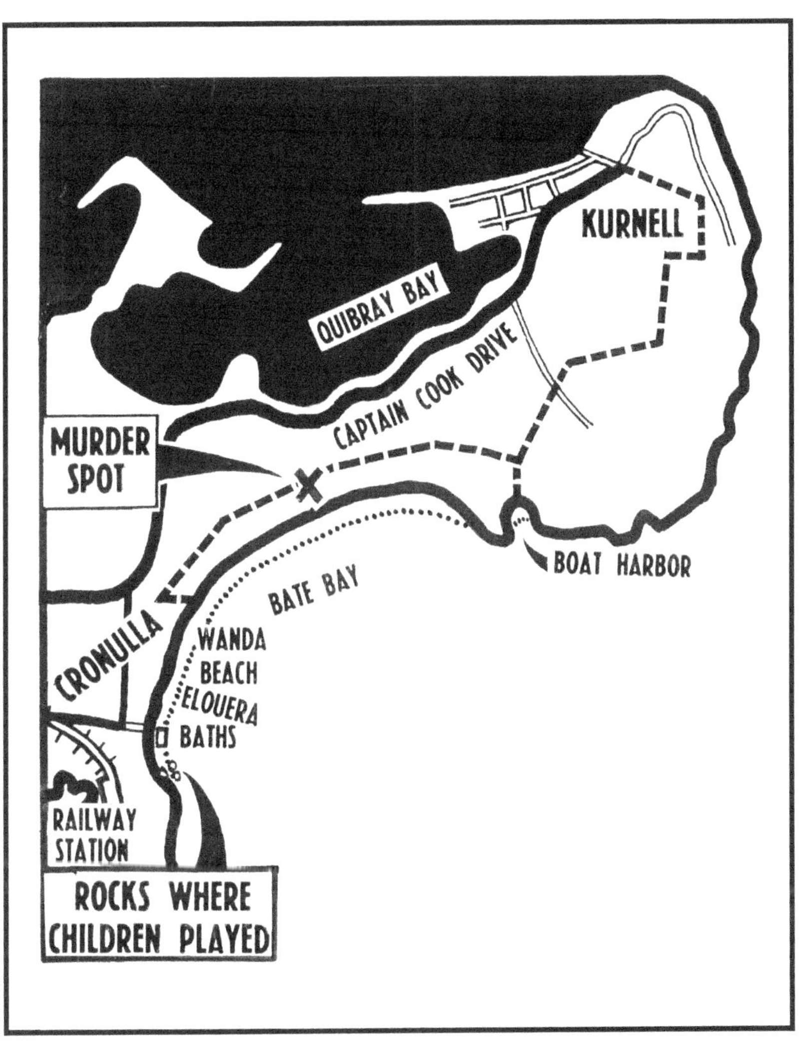

Above: An artist's map of the Cronulla area, showing the relevant areas of the children's outing to the beach on 11 January 1965.

Above: The scene that Peter Smith and his nephews stumbled upon on 12 January 1965 ... the partially exposed head and feet of 'a body'.

Above: Sydney detectives survey the crime scene. 'The body' is partially exposed in the foreground ... 'nature's grim illusion' that hid the reality of two bodies, 12 January 1965.

Above: Members of the Police Rescue Squad, plain-clothed detectives and local police commence their search of the Wanda sandhills, 12 January 1965.

Above left: The clothing Marianne Schmidt was wearing the day she was murdered: a black one-piece swimming costume and a multi-coloured sleeveless blouse.

Above right: The clothing Christine Sharrock was wearing the day she was murdered: a green-and-white patterned sleeveless blouse and white shorts.

Left and below:
The forensic search of
the surroundings was
earnest but lacked
sophistication. Police
begin the mammoth
task of hand-sifting the
tons of sand surrounding
the crime scene,
12 January 1965.

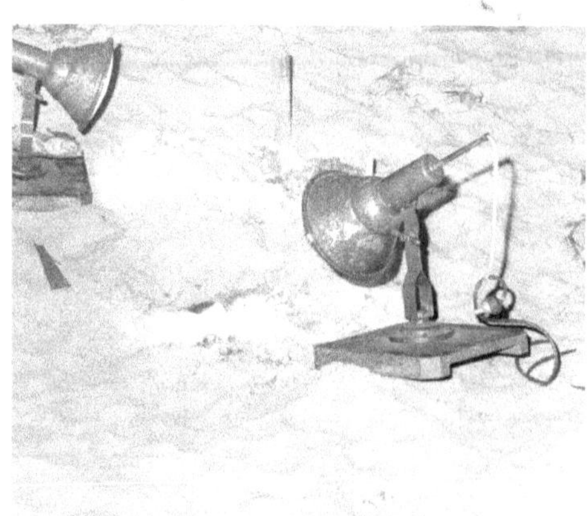

Left: Police Rescue
Squad floodlights do
their best to illuminate
the crime scene on the
evening of 12 January
1965, the day the girls'
bodies were found.

Above: This crude, handmade cross was erected by an unknown person on one of the nearby sandhills following the discovery of the bodies of Christine Sharrock and Marianne Schmidt at Wanda Beach.

CHAPTER 4
THE CRIME SCENE

'Wanda is a windswept, unprotected area of beach. It was a bit of an outpost even back then. If it wasn't a nice day, people would stay at the southern end of Cronulla near the rocks for protection. It's hard to speculate what drew the two young girls more than a mile past the clubhouse on such a windy day.'
Barry Ezzy, the former lifeguard who was on duty at Wanda Beach on 11 and 12 January 1965[1]

On the morning of Tuesday, 12 January 1965, with the fate of the two missing girls still unknown, Sergeant Robert Fulton of the Ryde police went to Brush Road, West Ryde, to follow up on the previous night's report that two girls had gone missing in the sandhills near Wanda Beach. When he arrived at the home of Jeanette Taig, Sergeant Fulton asked if she had heard from the girls.

'No, I thought that the police might have news', she said. Fulton then asked the elderly woman if the girls had boyfriends or had had any previous trouble with strangers.

'No. Christine knows how to look after herself. She had a very nasty experience about a year ago at Seven Hills', her grandmother said. Christine had been waiting at Seven Hills railway station when a man exposed himself to her, so she had quickly walked away.

When the sergeant asked Mrs Taig what she knew of the Schmidt family, she responded:

Mr Schmidt died about six months ago, and Mrs Schmidt is in hospital. The girl [Marianne] is looking after them ... there is a boy, Helmut, aged sixteen and ... employed, [who] is down the street shopping now. There is Hans, Peter, a girl Beatrice and two more boys.

Mrs Taig also told Sergeant Fulton that she had looked in on the children and 'they are doing all right for themselves'.

When Fulton went next door to the Schmidt residence, Hans told him the family had two cheques, for £16 and £12 respectively, which the children were to use in an emergency. Hans told Fulton he did not go to the beach with the others on 11 January because he needed to stay home and mow the lawn. Peter Schmidt was washing dishes at the time of Sergeant Fulton's visit, and when asked what had happened to Christine and Marianne the previous day, the boy responded:

It was very windy and the sand was cutting our legs and faces. The girls said we will go over to the sandhills and we left our things on the rocks and we found a place in the sandhills and then Marianne said, 'We will go back and get the things'. The two girls left us. They did not come back. We waited a long time, then we went and got our things and got the train and came home.

Sergeant Fulton found ample food in the Schmidt household and said that he would come back the following day and check on the children. As he left the Schmidt house, he heard Mrs Taig asking Trixie Schmidt to 'tell us what happened yesterday'. Trixie, just nine years old at the time, became very upset and could not answer.

There was still no immediate concern at this stage — the girls were simply lost. But the mood was soon to change. At

2.30 that afternoon, a body of a young female was found at Wanda Beach.

✝

At 2.40 p.m. on Tuesday, 12 January, Constable Ted Larsen was working at his desk at Cronulla police station when the phone rang. Larsen heard the person on the other end of the line take a deep breath as his words tumbled out and ran together. 'There's a body in the sand, a girl', the voice stuttered. 'I think she's dead.'[2]

Uniformed police were quickly dispatched to Wanda Surf Club, where they met Peter Smith, the seventeen-year-old youth who had made the phone call, and Barry Ezzy, a 23-year-old local lifeguard.

Ezzy, now retired, was interviewed for this book in October 2002 and remembered the day teenager Peter Smith came stumbling into the Wanda Surf Club: 'He was pretty distressed'.

Ezzy's brief as a beach inspector was, as he described it, to:

> *look after the surfing public, perform rescues when required and generally maintain law and order on the beach. Wanda was a one-man operation … If you had to save someone, you had to do it on your own because the council, in its wisdom, only employed one person on duty per beach. We each did a week's duty on each beach — Cronulla, North Cronulla and Wanda. Elouera Beach wasn't operating then.*

When the police arrived at the clubhouse Peter Smith took them to where he had found 'the body', while Ezzy remained at the clubhouse with Smith's three nephews. 'If someone drowned while I was away, there'd be some serious questions asked', he says with ironic understatement, considering a dead body had been found buried on his beach.

Peter Smith had recently travelled down to Sydney from the New South Wales Central Coast to search for work, and was staying in Caringbah with his married sister. On 11 January, Smith attended a 10.00 a.m. job interview in Marrickville before returning in the early afternoon to his sister's house, where he had lunch with his nephews. The following day, he decided to take his three young nephews — brothers Bill (aged seven) and Jim (aged five), and Stewart (aged eight), the son of his other sister — to Cronulla for the day. Unlike the previous day, Tuesday, 12 January was a beautiful summer's day. Catching the train to Cronulla at about 10.00 a.m., Smith and his nephews had lunch and then decided to go for a walk to the sandhills, where they spent some time playing.

'The younger boys were restless and wanted to go for a walk up to the sandhills', Smith recalled in a November 2002 interview for this book. 'We ended up about one-and-a-half miles past the Wanda Surf Club. On the way back, we were walking in behind the first row of sandhills about 150 yards from the water's edge.' Smith was carrying his youngest nephew now because the boy was tired, while the other boys were running ahead of him and doubling back.

'One of my nephews had stopped in one of the valleys of a sandhill and we noticed something in the sand pretty much at the same time', Smith recalled. On their present track the boys were heading towards what appeared to be a store mannequin that someone had thrown away or buried in the sand:

As I walked towards it I could see some feet sticking out of a pile of sand and the partly exposed head and hair of a person. I scraped some of the sand away from the head and with the long hair exposed I realised that it was the body of a female.

When Peter Smith discovered the crime scene he thought there was just one body buried in the sand — nature's grim illusion, linking the head of one girl's body to the heels of another.

Smith gathered his three nephews and walked back in the direction of the Wanda Surf Club. Rampant thoughts overtook him … was she a drowning victim? No, it was too far from the water. The young boys were asking questions now. What was it? A body, he told them. He looked for a house so he could sound the alarm but there were no houses backing onto the Wanda area, only rolling hills and scrubland. The Wanda Surf Club was the nearest building he could find.

Smith took his nephews to the surf club residence and found Barry Ezzy on duty. Smith used the telephone to contact the Cronulla police, and later directed a constable and several detectives to the place where 'the body' lay. 'I don't know the area very well and it wasn't until I spoke to the caretaker at the surf club that I realised it was Wanda Beach', Smith told the detectives. 'It was about twelve months ago that I was at Cronulla Beach and it has been a couple of years since I was up in the sandhills.' The 'grave' was about one-and-a-quarter miles north of the Wanda Surf Club, in the hollow of a sandhill extending from the top of a dune and pointing downward toward the beach. Avoiding the dry sand around the makeshift grave, the detectives quickly determined that there were two bodies buried; the head of one body and the right elbow and heels of the other had been exposed by the wind. 'The detectives were in their full suits and looked strangely out of place on the beach', Smith said. 'Then one of them said, "There's three feet here".[2] The full horror of what was buried was then revealed.

Of the many detectives drawn to the crime scene the day the bodies were found — some to survey the surroundings, others to 'just have a look'[3] — was Detective Sergeant Keith Paull. In 1965 Paull was in his mid-forties and one of the more experienced crime investigators stationed at the Sydney CIB (Criminal Investigation Bureau). Paull was joined by Detective Sergeant Eric Humphreys and a number of other detectives, including Jack Lucas and Barry Reynolds, under the direction of Detective Inspector Ned Haines, who took charge of the case.

After searching the dunes and nearby seashore, investigators noted that a grave had not been dug at all; the sand had simply been heaped over the two bodies where they lay. With the light beginning to fade, detectives conscripted independent news photographer Geoff Jessop to take photographs of the crime scene,[4] and a plaster cast was made of a man's shoeprint that had been left in the sand next to the grave. When the sand was removed from the top of the grave in the presence of two government medical officers — Doctors Laing and Brighton — the positioning of the bodies became clear. Marianne Schmidt was lying on her right side in a semi-foetal position, her left leg bent at the knee at a right angle to her body. Christine Sharrock was lying face down in the sand, her right arm bent at the elbow, her forearm close to her face as if shielding herself. The bodies were in line with each other, with Christine's head touching Marianne's feet.

Marianne was wearing a black one-piece swimming costume that had a white lace front; the crotch of the costume had been cut in the front and pulled up around her breasts. Over her costume was a multi-coloured sleeveless blouse. Christine was wearing a white brassiere underneath a green-and-white patterned sleeveless blouse that had a zip fastener. Her legs were slightly apart and her bloodstained white shorts had been thrust into her crotch; a sanitary belt and pad had been removed and placed on the right side of her buttocks. Both girls were shoeless.

Christine was also wearing a heart-shaped locket, gold bracelet, gold signet ring with the initials 'BT' engraved on it and pierced gold earrings. Robbery was quickly discounted as a motive for the murders, and no item had been taken by the killer as a 'trophy'.

Detectives noted a drag mark — 112 feet long — extending north in the sand away from Christine's body and down an incline leading to a gully between two sand dunes. Blood was found in the sand and grass stalks along the drag mark, and police stated in their reports that these bloodstains were consistent with Christine's body being dragged toward the grave. Detectives found bloodstains covered by sand at intervals of approximately ten feet, but could not ascertain whether these bloodstains had been deliberately covered by the killer or had been covered by the elements.

Police could only speculate how the girls encountered their killer. Were they befriended or simply set upon? At what point did Christine run away? As police moved and photographed the bodies of Christine and Marianne, the extent of the girls' injuries become apparent and detectives began to piece together a scenario of how the girls died. Police surmised that as Marianne lay dead or dying, Christine attempted to flee but was caught by the killer and struck from behind with a blunt object. The killer then subdued her with another blow to the chin and stabbed her in the back as he dragged her to where Marianne lay. The killer attempted to rape Christine, removing her sanitary belt and napkin and shoving her shorts into her crotch area. The physical evidence showed that Christine's eyes were blackened, her face was misshapen as if violently punched and an abrasion was clearly visible under her chin. Marianne's throat had been cut, the callousness of the act sickening to the hardened detectives. (It was later reported by the press that a knife had been 'violently plunged into her throat' and her head 'almost severed'[5] but these were exaggerations of a nevertheless terrible injury.) There were obvious signs of other stab wounds and it was apparent to the detectives at the crime scene that Marianne had also been sexually molested.

Doctors ascertained that the girls had died within half an hour of each other; they had similar body temperatures and rigor mortis had not set in due to the bodies being kept warm in the sand over the twenty-four hours following their deaths.

The police soon set out to identify the two bodies. At 4.30 p.m. on Tuesday, 12 January, Detective Inspector Newman from Cronulla police station visited the Taig and Schmidt residences in Brush Road, West Ryde, in order to obtain as much information as possible about Christine and Marianne, especially the clothing worn by the girls the day they went missing. Newman arrived in the company of Sergeant Green from Ryde police station and spoke to members of the Schmidt family first, in their front yard, but did not inform the Schmidt children that two bodies had been found. As Newman went next door to the Taig residence, Sergeant Green spoke with Wolfgang Schmidt.

Wolfgang told Sergeant Green that when Christine and Marianne had left for their walk, he 'went up the hill after them and they were walking away and there was a fat boy walking with them, between the two girls'. This was the first time any of the children had mentioned anyone walking with the girls on the afternoon they went missing. Wolfgang went on to describe the boy as 'fat and had nothing on except his trousers … they were light grey long trousers and he had a towel, blue-coloured over his shoulders and fair hair'.

'How big was the boy who was with your sister?', Green prodded. 'He was about as big as the boys who go to high school.'

'How far … [were] the fat boy and the girls from you when you saw him with them?'

Wolfgang indicated a distance of about 120 feet.

While police were questioning the Taig and Schmidt families, Hans Schmidt was visiting his mother in hospital. Mrs Schmidt had expected Helmut and Hans to visit her — Helmut planned to visit his mother then catch a 10.00 p.m. train to Temora, where the family once lived, for a three-day holiday — and when she asked Hans why he had come alone, he told her that Helmut had stayed at home to finish painting the kitchen.

'What did Marianne do today?' Mrs Schmidt asked. 'What did she cook for lunch and did she have washday?'

'I cooked fried potatoes and scrambled eggs', Hans responded enthusiastically.

'Why did not Marianne cook the dinner?' asked Mrs Schmidt.

'You know I have to tell you', he said. 'The boys [*sic*] came home about nine o'clock yesterday evening but the girls did not come home.'

Worry gave way to fear. Hans made three phone calls to Mrs Taig during the visiting hour on Tuesday night to see if the girls had arrived home, but there was no sign of them. Mrs Schmidt told the nursing sister on duty that night that Marianne and her friend had not returned from Cronulla Beach the day before and asked the nurse to make sure that any message concerning the girls was passed to her, even if it was in the middle of the night.

At 6.15 p.m. that day, detectives cordoned off the crime

scene at Wanda Beach and commenced their forensic investigation. By sunset, only a preliminary search of the area could be completed and the Police Rescue Squad erected floodlights to illuminate the crime scene. As night fell, the sandhills became a hive of activity — about 100 people were ordered away from the crime scene while the bodies were being examined. It was reported that police repeatedly warned several teenage girls and an elderly woman to move away while they exhumed the bodies. Although the floodlights were not powerful enough to allow for an extensive search of the area, detectives continued throughout the night and into the following morning.

Barry Ezzy was training on the beach after finishing his shift and was an interested observer. 'We used to train hard for our R&R [rescue and resuscitation] events', Ezzy recalled in a 2002 interview. 'That night we had training on the beach while the police investigation was underway and you could see the floodlights lighting up the sandhills.' Silhouettes of suited detectives flickered in and out of the dunes. At this stage Ezzy did not know that two bodies had been found.

Shortly after 7.30 p.m., the Police Rescue Squad brought a four-wheel drive along a track to within fifty yards of the crime scene, to be used as a makeshift hearse. A Rescue Squad sergeant and senior constable wrapped the girls' bodies in blankets and carried them on stretchers to the vehicle. Later that night, the bodies were identified by Leslie Taig, Christine Sharrock's uncle. After a brief conversation with Detective Sergeant Paull at 9.30 p.m. at Cronulla police station, Les Taig, from the suburb of Ermington, went with Paull and Detective Sergeants Cully and Humphreys to an enclosed yard on the premises, where he viewed the bodies. He identified the dark-haired girl as Marianne Schmidt; he had known her for about two years and she lived in Brush

Road. He then identified the fair-haired girl as Christine Sharrock, the daughter of his sister, Beryl Maher.

Taig told the detectives that he had last seen his niece alive at about 9.30 p.m. on Sunday, 10 January at his mother's house where Christine lived. That evening, Taig had a conversation with both girls regarding their plans to take the younger Schmidt children to Cronulla Beach the following day. He had not heard anything more about the issue until Mrs Taig rang him at 7.00 a.m. on Tuesday to say that Christine and Marianne had not returned home with the other children the previous night and that she had reported the girls missing.

Now that the positive identification had been made, the families of the deceased were notified. Mrs Schmidt was told at 11.30 p.m. by Doctor Atkinson, the Medical Superintendent at King George V Hospital, informing her that Christine and Marianne had been found.

'But not alive', Mrs Schmidt said.

'If you think that, it is true', was his reply. He said nothing further and did not disclose the circumstances of their deaths.

During the night, the girls' bodies were transferred to the city morgue. At about 9.00 a.m. the following day, Detective Selwood formally presented and identified the bodies to Doctor Laing. Detective Sergeant Lindsay of the Scientific Bureau then took detailed photographs of the bodies before Doctors Laing and Brighton conducted the post-mortem examination.

The autopsy revealed that Christine Sharrock had suffered a fractured skull and multiple knife wounds — a stab wound near the right shoulder blade, one behind the right ear, three to the right side of the back above the waistline, one to the right side of the back at the neck, two small cuts to the right side of the back just below the other wounds and one small cut below the neck wound. There were also six roughly parallel cuts across the front of her neck; these cuts were superficial, being $\frac{1}{16}$ inch deep and $\frac{1}{16}$ inch wide, and were consistent with the serrated edge of a fishing knife being scraped across the skin of her neck. However, the wound behind the left ear was described as 'gaping' — $\frac{1}{2}$ inch wide with a $\frac{3}{4}$-inch track. Both eyes were badly bruised, distorting her facial features; there was an abrasion on her chin (on the right side of the jaw); and bruising to the inside of her lip. There were also two scratches on the calf muscle of her right leg.

Doctor Laing was of the opinion that Christine's skull had been fractured with a blunt object, possibly a piece of wood, a rock, a length of water pipe or a similar instrument. The injury was the result of a heavy blow over the right optical region, which left her cranium full of blood. A stab wound had pierced her liver and several had penetrated her lungs, which were also full of blood. Christine's death was deemed to be the result of multiple injuries, because the order of the injuries could not be ascertained. The stab wounds were inflicted with a knife that was sharp on one side and blunt on the other. The wounds ranged from 13 to 15 millimetres in width but tapered off towards their maximum depth. It was determined that, as the maximum depth of Christine's wounds was $2\frac{1}{2}$ inches, the blade was at least this length.

Although Christine's hymen was intact, there was evidence of a recent abrasion to the external genitals, which suggested that intercourse had been attempted but was not of sufficient depth to rupture the hymen. Though no male sperm could be detected, a vaginal swab was sent for analysis, as were samples of Christine's blood, pubic and head hair. It was discovered that Christine had a blood alcohol level of 0.015; enough for her to have consumed a 10-ounce glass of beer. The professional opinion of Doctor E 'Sam' Ogg, who conducted his own tests, was that, although it was possible that food content in her stomach had fermented and contributed to an alcohol reading, the alcohol had been consumed orally. This finding was supported by the results of two standard forensic procedures: a titration test and a gas chromatograph test.

When Doctor Laing examined Christine's stomach contents to help establish the time of her death, he detected cabbage and celery in an indigested form; as no meat was present the doctor surmised that Christine may have eaten part of a Chinese meal. In later reports, however, the contents were more generally referred to as 'vegetable matter'. Doctor Laing conjectured that, as the food was only slightly digested, death could have occurred immediately after the food consumption or at the most, up to one hour afterwards.

The post-mortem examination of Marianne Schmidt's body revealed that she had also suffered various stab wounds, the result of a frenzied attack. Her body had two stab wounds to the outside of the left upper arm, two to the inside of the left arm, two to the side of the left breast, one to the left side of the back, three to the middle of the back, three to the right side of the back, one to the left shoulderblade and a large, deep laceration to the front of the throat. There was also one small fingernaillike' scratch to Marianne's left thigh about 2 inches below her swimming costume suntan mark.

One of the stab wounds had penetrated Marianne's left breast, travelled between two of her ribs and punctured her heart; Doctor Laing maintained that this wound caused Marianne's death. It was obvious to the doctors and detectives present during the autopsy that the knife that inflicted these injuries had also caused the death of Christine Sharrock. The deepest wound, the one that penetrated Marianne's heart, was about 3 inches deep, but considering the 'elasticity in the organs encountered', the knife that inflicted this wound was more likely about 2½ inches in length.

The bottom part of Marianne's swimming costume had been cut across the pelvic area, exposing her external genitals. The cut was jagged and the bottom of the costume was pulled up around her breasts. Marianne Schmidt's hymen was also intact, but there was evidence of a recent abrasion to the 'private part' and a 'sticky substance' was found 'therein'. A swab was taken and a number of male spermatozoa were later found to be present.

An examination was made of Marianne's stomach and found that it was empty except for a black fluid identified as congealed blood. It was clear that Marianne had not eaten for some time. There was no alcohol in her blood, which, considering both girls ate a similar luncheon meal, supported Doctor Ogg's view that Christine Sharrock may have taken alcohol orally. Doctor Brighton later indicated that if Marianne had eaten a sandwich of Marmite or cucumber, as was suggested by her siblings, it would have taken approximately 1½–2 hours for it to fully digest to a liquid state, and 2–3 hours for her stomach to empty of the liquid matter. No trace of tomato skin was found in Marianne's stomach, which Doctor Brighton would have expected if she had consumed tomato sandwiches, because, according to his forensic report, tomato skin is not destroyed by digestion but excreted through the organs.

This evidence showed that Marianne had died a minimum of 2–3 hours after sharing the lunch that she had made for her siblings before they started their walk to the Wanda Beach sandhills. The time of death — estimated to be no later than midnight on Monday, 11 January — was arrived at through an examination of the post-mortem staining of the bodies.

At Wanda Beach police kept guard at the murder scene overnight until first light on Wednesday, 13 January. Police from nearby divisional stations then searched a radius of approximately half a mile out from where the bodies were found. At first, under the direction of a detective sergeant from the Police Scientific Branch, police painstakingly sifted the fine sand around the shallow graves within a radius of thirty yards; they then moved on to the coarse sand further out. The search was carried out by twentytwo police from six divisions as well as the Police Rescue Squad. A large crowd that had gathered following the broadcasting of news of the discovery was again kept well away from the crime scene by police.

Police began the mammoth task of sifting through hundreds of tons of sand around the dunes where the girls' bodies were found; they were searching for the presumed murder weapons — a fishing knife and a blunt instrument. A tractor towing an 8-inch rake and a council front-end loader (tip truck) cleared the sand to a depth of 18 inches and by noon 200 tons had been sifted through a makeshift sieve. Detectives wearing singlets, shorts and their distinctive brown hats searched the sand by hand as it poured out of the funnel of the tip truck and, although there was much earnestness in their approach, by today's standards there was not a lot of sophistication.

Over the course of several days, the dunes surrounding the grave were dotted with police markers where particular items had been found. Various items of old clothing, three knives and a striped towel were found; none of the items found, however, were related to the murder. Two of the three knives found near Wanda Beach were traced back to local fishermen; the third knife, which was too broad to be the murder weapon, was sent for scientific examination. The day the girls' bodies were discovered, a Cronulla man found a pair of black flippers by the water's edge half a mile north of Wanda Beach; these flippers were to become an important part of one police scenario of what may have happened that day. The crime scene was pored over for the remainder of the week.

By Friday, 15 January, a homemade cross fashioned out of wood and seaweed mysteriously appeared in a small hillock overlooking the gravesite. On 19 January at about 12.30 p.m., while searching the sandhills near where the bodies were discovered, Sergeant Tyson of the Police Rescue Squad found a piece of steel — a section of knife blade about $\frac{9}{10}$ inch by $\frac{8}{10}$ inch in length, broken at both ends and stained. The piece of steel was sent for further testing, which determined that 'stains present on the knife gave positive presumptive tests for blood'. The forensic certificate also noted that 'insufficient stains were present for further tests to be carried out'.

On 25 January, Max Hatherley, a metallurgist from the University of New South Wales, examined the partial blade. In his official report, Mr Hatherley found the blade to be of a high quality stainless steel used in the manufacture of high-grade carving knives or surgical instruments, and was probably manufactured in Europe or the United States. The knife most resembling the piece of blade was a kitchen knife; tests carried out by Mr Hatherley confirmed that if such a knife was thrust into a hard, 'penetration-resistant' material such as a shoulderblade, it could fracture in a way consistent with the partial blade found. This type of knife was therefore considered the most likely murder weapon.

Despite extensive inquiries among importers, a knife that satisfied the requirements of the suspected murder weapon could not be found. The piece of blade was entered into evidence and tagged as Exhibit Number 23 at the City Coroner's Court for the coronial inquest the following April. It was the only piece of physical evidence ever found in the sandhills.

CHAPTER 5

MEDIA WARS

'The massive police hunt today for the "Wanda Beach sex murderer" is being concentrated on a mysterious, long-haired youth. Women at Wanda, near Cronulla, are in terror at the thought that the homicidal pervert could still be wandering about the sandhills. The savageness of the attack on two defenceless and innocent girls enjoying a day at the beach has shocked the community.'

Bill Jenkins writing in the Daily Mirror, *13 January 1965*

As Australians sat down to their evening meal on Tuesday, 12 January 1965, the first reports of the discovery of two bodies on a Sydney beach began to filter through the television news services. Film crews scurried to get their footage to air, filmed in shadowy black-and-white during this pre-video era. The Sydney commercial stations, ATN 7 and TCN 9, carried sketchy reports on their 6.30 p.m. bulletins before the national broadcaster, ABC Channel 2, provided a more detailed account at 7.00 p.m. Every parent's nightmare was being brought into Australian lounge rooms: two fifteen-year-old girls murdered, possibly raped and buried in the sand of a popular Sydney beach at the height of the summer holidays.

Sydneysiders awoke the following morning to the banner headline 'TWO TEENAGE GIRLS RAPED, MURDERED' splashed over the front page of the morning tabloid. The 13 January edition of the *Daily Telegraph* began:

A man yesterday found the bodies of two fifteen-year-old girls who had been raped and murdered, then buried in sand at Wanda Beach.

The girls had been stabbed several times and their bodies savagely slashed.

A trail of blood indicated that their nearby nude bodies had been dragged about 30 yards before being buried in the side of a sand dune. They were buried one in front of the other in an L-shaped depression scooped out of the sand.

A Cronulla man, Peter Smith, about 28 [sic], found the grave about 2.30 p.m. yesterday.

Police said he was walking over the sand dunes with three young nephews. He saw bloodstains in the sand. He followed the blood about 30 yards towards the sea.

On the side of the sand dune he saw a girl's long hair and two feet protruding from a mound.

He ran more than a mile over soft sand back to Wanda Surf Club to telephone police. Detectives reached the place where the bodies were found shortly before 3 p.m.

They scooped away the sand with their hands and makeshift trowels.

They found one girl lying face down in the sand. She had been stabbed at least three times in the back. She was wearing only a blouse. Torn, bloodstained shorts were between her legs.

The other girl, whose head and part of her body apparently had been exposed by the wind, shifting the sand, lay on her side. She had on only the torn upper part of a dress. She had been stabbed in her chest, throat and back and slashed across the stomach.

A knife had been plunged into her throat.

Later that day, the girls' names were released, as were details of their trip to the beach and the time they were reported missing.

The evening newspaper, the *Sun*, led off its 13 January edition with:

> *Detectives investigating the knife murder of two school girls whose bodies were found at Wanda Beach yesterday, are searching for a sixteen-year-old surfie with long, blond hair.*
>
> *The youth was seen talking to the girls shortly before the time they are believed to have been killed. His description has been circulated to all Sydney police.*
>
> *Another surfer gave them the information — he saw a youth talking to the girls at the northern end of Wanda beach shortly before they disappeared and watched them talking to the youth for five minutes.*

This was either a cover to protect the witness's identity or pure guesswork on the newspaper's part; the clue concerning the chief suspect had come from Wolfgang Schmidt. The report continued:

> *Detective Inspector Haines called newsmen to a special conference at Cronulla police station to tell them of the breakthrough in the police investigation and to give details of the youth's appearance.*

The *Sun*'s description circulated of the prime suspect — 'age sixteen, medium height and build, light coloured long hair, wearing only long grey trousers … body and face … suntanned and … white anti-sunburn cream on his nose' — became the description confirmed in the minds of the public; the image of a teenage, blond-haired 'surfie type' was locked into place. Thousands of young men resembled this description and many of them, from scruffy teenagers to school kids, immediately came under suspicion.

Continuing its 13 January report, the *Sun* theorised, incorrectly, that:

> *a maniac stabbed one girl in the back, killing her. He then chased the other girl, raped her and stabbed her.*
>
> *The attacker could have parked a car in any of the dozen tracks leading off Captain Cook Drive into the edge of the sandhills.*
>
> *The bodies were found in an isolated area seldom used by swimmers or surfboard riders … a mile from Captain Cook Drive and several hundred yards from the nearest trafficable track.*

Sydney crime reporter Bill Jenkins, a well-known and experienced journalist who had covered many of Australia's most notorious crimes including the 'Pyjama Girl' case, the 'Shark Arm' case and the 'Graham Thorne kidnapping' case,[1] did not shy away from reporting the more sordid aspects of the crime scene in his 13 January *Daily Mirror* report:

> *Drag marks indicate that the first girl's body was dragged up to the spot where the second one was lying dead or dying.*
>
> *Christine had stab wounds in the back and it was thought that they were inflicted as the murderer caught up with her.*
>
> *Marianne was first to be struck down at the spot where they found bloodstains in the sand. They think Christine probably ran away screaming in terror but no one would have heard her in the remote area.*
>
> *One girl's head was almost severed by a knife plunged*

violently into her throat. Her swimsuit was slashed up around her chest.

Another girl's bloodstained shorts had been torn off and thrust between her legs.

Jenkins first referred to the crime as 'The Dunes Murders' but this handle did not stick with the public. Almost immediately, the deaths of Christine Sharrock and Marianne Schmidt became known as 'The Wanda Beach Murders'.

Journalist Steve Raymond, who in January 1965 was a twenty-year-old news reporter with the top-rating Sydney radio station, 2SM, also covered the Wanda crime. Raymond went on to become one of Australia's most respected journalists and broadcasters following a thirty-plus-year career in which he covered world events such as the assassination of Robert F. Kennedy, then went on to help found the western Sydney radio station 2WS, where he was director of Current Affairs for twenty years before moving to 2UE. In a May 2003 interview for this book, Raymond recalled:

The Wanda Beach double murder was a huge story; such outrages were almost unheard of in those fairly innocent times. I remember covering police news conferences, visiting Marianne Schmidt's home in Brush Road, West Ryde, and vividly recall one weekend retracing the path taken by the girls from Cronulla station into the sandhills north of Wanda … [it was] a very eerie experience. But almost a year on, there was no breakthrough, although it seemed every afternoon tabloid were reporting some startling Wanda Beach development or breakthrough. Those false alarms — or 'beat-ups', to be more accurate — caused untold heartbreak.

The press quickly descended on the Brush Road homes of the two girls. While the elderly Taig family refused to give interviews, the Schmidt children were cooperative to the point of naïveté. Their story — they were the children of German immigrants; they had tragically lost their father the previous year; they were fending for themselves while their mother was in hospital — was a newspaper owner's dream. When reporters visited the family home the day after the bodies were identified, they found Helmut Schmidt shouldering the burden of his sister's death. In its 13 January report, the *Sun* reported Helmut as saying: 'Mum is very sick in hospital and doesn't know what happened. The doctors have told me I must not break the news to her yet'. When asked if his brothers and sister knew what had happened, Helmut added: 'I can't tell them. They have talked to the police but still don't know what's going on.' Police had told Helmut and Hans, but not the younger children, of the girls' deaths.

Social workers at King George V Hospital — where Mrs Schmidt was recovering from surgery — arranged domestic assistance for the Schmidt family, but for the week until their mother was well enough to return home the children existed on the kindness of both neighbours and strangers. 'People have been good', Helmut Schmidt told the press, as reported in the 14 January edition of the *Sun*. 'That's why we'll get along somehow. It was wonderful when people started bringing food for us.' Dozens of neighbours, friends and well-wishers helped the Schmidt family through the next week, including the West Ryde Lions Club, the Lutheran Church and The Smith Family. In the midst of the tragic situation the Schmidt family became a cause célèbre.

While the Schmidt children became known to the public, the Taig family grieved in private. There was a lot of criticism of the media within Christine Sharrock's family, which felt that the Schmidt children were showered with attention. The Taigs did not want media attention, but felt the grief of both families was shared equally and were critical of the disproportionate amount of attention focused on the Schmidt family. The girls could not be separated in life but their deaths and the subsequent media coverage drove a wedge between the neighbouring families. Factual errors in many media reports only compounded the pain — one newspaper even juxtaposed the girls' names under the wrong photographs; this, according to Margaret Kavazos, particularly hurt Christine's grandmother.[2]

The newspapers did try to play their part in the investigation, asking all drycleaners to report any evidence of bloodstained clothing (Campsie police contacted Wanda Beach investigators regarding one such drycleaning shop but the lead was quickly discounted), publishing descriptions of suspects police wanted to question and finally carrying appeals from the police when the investigation went cold. The 15 January edition of the *Sun* reported CIB Chief Superintendent Ron Walden's appeal to 'every swimmer and sunbather [at Wanda Beach on 11 January] to contact police so that the death scene on the day could be re-created', and asked the public to contact Cronulla police or call the police emergency number with any information.

Some reporters were so close to the story they sometimes became the story. On the day after the bodies of Christine and Marianne were found, Dimity Torbett, a reporter for the *Daily Mirror*, was with photographer Barry Ward at Wanda Beach as a group of teenagers, many fitting Wolfgang Schmidt's description of the suspect, was milling around the crime scene. Ward noticed a blond-haired youth, about 5 feet 9 inches tall with a thin build, suntanned face, wearing a fawn windcheater and lightcoloured trousers that were noticeably bloodstained. Ward took the boy's photograph and he and Torbett reported the matter to the police. Ward's photograph was circulated among detectives, and the boy in the photograph was later tracked down and cleared of any involvement in the crime. The stains on his trousers were not bloodstains and he was not even at Wanda Beach the day the girls died.

Reporters from opposing newspapers continually tried to outdo each other. At 6.30 p.m. on Thursday, 14 January, a woman was walking along the beach at North Cronulla when she found a pocketknife with a 4-inch blade. Police noted in their running sheet from that day that the knife was 'in old condition' and 'not bloodstained in any way'. The *Sun*'s 14 January banner headline dominated most of its front page:

KNIFE FOUND

Detectives are now examining a knife found on a beach near where two teenage girls were killed in the dunes on Monday afternoon. A blond surfie who walked into the sandhills with the victims is now being hunted by the police.

The distinctive wounds in the girls' bodies pointed to a fishing knife with a serrated edge as the murder weapon, not a smooth-edged pocketknife. The *Sun*'s misleading headline was quickly debunked by its rival the *Daily Mirror* in its 14 January edition:

A small penknife was found today two miles from the murder scene. The woman who found it handed it to police. Detectives at Cronulla completely discounted the knife as the murder weapon. They said a report in the Sun *about the knife today was completely misleading and damaging to police inquiries.*

The next day, 15 January 1965, the *Sun* topped itself with the following:

BOY HELD

An 18-year-old boy with long, blond 'surfie' hair is being held for questioning at Brisbane CIB.

The full story (reported in the same article) was that the youth in question was in Sydney on Monday, 11 January and had subsequently hitchhiked to Brisbane. When detained, he was found with three knives in his possession — a 3-inch serrated blade; a broad-bladed 10-inch throwing knife; and a sheath knife with a 4-inch blade. The youth was remanded in a Brisbane court for one week on a charge of possessing stolen property but nothing else — particularly nothing related to the Wanda Beach murders — came from his interrogation.

The *Sun* had also reported, in its 13 January edition, the grave fears held for the safety of two Canberra schoolgirls who had gone missing from a Nowra camping ground on New Year's Eve. When the girls turned up safely in the north Sydney suburb of Chatswood twelve days later, they informed detectives investigating the Wanda Beach murders that they had hitchhiked to Cronulla — not far from where Christine and Marianne were murdered — and slept on the beach before moving on to a boarding house in the eastern suburbs of Sydney. The girls were interviewed but could shed no light on the Wanda investigation and were returned to their worried parents.

Although undoubtedly frustrated by the inaccurate and exaggerated reporting, police used the media as a tool to obtain information they needed from the public. On 21 January, the *Sun* reported an announcement by detectives regarding eight people they wanted to question who were at

Wanda Beach on the day of the murders:

- a man who stood up in the sand, shook sand from his body, trunks and towel and walked towards the Wanda Surf Club;
- two boys playing in the sandhills;
- a motorist in a utility truck who helped a woman free her sedan bogged in the sand near a track off Captain Cook Drive;
- two men rod-fishing on the beach;
- a sunbather who protected his head from the sun and the wind with a mask made from a tin box; and
- a blond youth — approximately sixteen years old — who walked into the sandhills at approximately 1.00 p.m.

Witnesses did begin to come forward but not the blond-haired youth Wolfgang Schmidt allegedly saw walking off into the sandhills with Christine and Marianne. Police could not discount the possibility that the youth may have had nothing to do with the murders but was now too scared to come forward; nor could they discount the notion that Wolfgang Schmidt, just seven years old, was mistaken and the youth did not exist at all. Detectives had been alerted to the existence of a 'serial beach pest' in the Wanda Beach area and used the media to ask women who had been approached by this person to come forward with any information that could help police begin the arduous task of piecing together descriptions of potential suspects.

By the middle of January public opinion was running hot and the local papers gave people the opportunity to vent their anger. In the 15 January 1965 edition of the *Daily Telegraph*, under the heading 'BRING BACK THE ROPE', a cross-section of letters expressed the range of powerful feelings sparked by the murders.

Mrs I Thomas of Panania wrote:

> *As a mother of small children, two of them girls, I am at a loss to understand the apathy of the law towards the rapists and murderers who are terrorising our community. I believe that capital punishment should be brought in to try and combat this evil in our community.*

C Keary of Blakehurst offered:

> *Obviously the Wanda Beach murderer may be mentally ill … some advocate killing these poor afflicted people but I wonder how many would similarly justify a doctor treating a physically ill patient by execution? To my mind, there is no real distinction between the guilt of a convicted murderer and the society which executes him.*

These comments must be considered in the context of an English justice system still reeling from the implications of a posthumous pardon awarded to Timothy Evans, who was hanged for the murder of his wife and child in England in the late 1950s. Years later John Christie, Evans' neighbour, pleaded guilty to the murders of Evans' family, his own wife and several other women who visited his flat in Kensington. Christie was hanged, but justice was too late for Timothy Evans.

J De Lissa of Cremorne Point argued:

> *At a time when the whole community is revolted by a terrible sex crime, it is difficult to appeal to reason, rather*

than emotion, but this is just what we must do. The execution of a criminal is an admission by society of failure.

G Burgoyne of McMahons Point asked:

In these (crimes), the guilty show their unfitness to be members of a civilised community and should be eliminated, as are diseased members of flocks and herds. It is true that the scaffold is a barbarous instrument ... could not an odourless gas be employed?

The State Upper House Member for Cronulla, the Honourable IR Griffiths, waded into the public debate and was quoted in a *Daily Telegraph* report on 22 January 1965 as stating that 'mounted police should patrol Wanda Beach to rid the area of hoodlum packs who made the sand dunes their headquarters'. Just which group of youths he was referring to — 'surfies', 'rockers' or the 'perverts' who frequented the sandhills — remained unclear. The public response to Wolfgang Schmidt's description of the blondhaired youth was overwhelming; the problem with the description, however, was that it was too vague to build up an identikit picture; it also matched a large proportion of male teens at the time. Over 100 calls from the public led to dead ends. And there were, of course, the prank confessions. An example was a sixteen-year-old youth, described in the *Daily Mirror* on 18 January 1965 as 'completely garrulous', who confessed to the murders before finally admitting that it was all 'a joke' — his mates dared him to do it.

In the media frenzy that exploded after the discovery of the bodies, much loose talk was bandied around about the morals of the two girls, including suggestions that they may have deliberately wandered into the sandhills of Wanda Beach looking for sex. Medical evidence showed that although the girls had been sexually assaulted — probably after they were killed — their hymens were still intact and both had died virgins. When this fact was released to the press, police went on the record and stated that the girls were of 'good character'; detectives assigned to the case even said that they would have 'been proud to have them as their daughters'[3] — the last public courtesy afforded the girls before their burial on 20 January.

The media covered the burials of both girls. Of Marianne Schmidt's funeral, Ron Saw, a popular columnist, wrote in the *Daily Mirror* on 21 January 1965:

> *'Service for the late Schmidt. Please sign the visitors' handbook on the right before going into the chapel.'*
>
> *To the man in the shiny black suit, she was no Marianne. She was simply 'the late Schmidt' … he had his job to do; for he was a busy, efficient, impersonal part of the Australian way of dying.*
>
> *Visitors at a funeral service. Surely not. Mourners and sympathisers in the chapel and, in a case like this, sightseers and ghouls in the street. But nobody visits a funeral!*

It was a time when everyone was forced to confront the best and the worst of the way the media covered the story. Most of the media coverage was factual, respectful of the families and ultimately helpful to the police investigation. But several reports, especially in the print media, were obtrusive, manipulative and patently wrong. A double murder, particularly of two teenage girls, was rare in the mid-1960s, and the press would not let the story go away.

'It gripped the public', said Bill Jenkins in an interview

shortly before his death. 'It excited terrific competition between the newspapers. There wasn't one other case I covered that surpassed it for public interest. A scoop on Wanda was a terrific seller — the editor demanded that we never keep our noses out of it.'[4]

On the night of 27 January, Wolfgang Schmidt was woken at 10.30, dressed by his mother and taken to Randwick police station to view suspects in a police line-up. Wolfgang's older brother Helmut and Detective Sergeant Keith Paull accompanied the seven-year-old. At the same time uniformed police swept through Coogee Beach and collected a dozen youths for a line-up, and detectives collected a seventeen-year-old youth from his nearby home for questioning before he was also placed in the line-up.

'I walked up and down but the boy wasn't there', Wolfgang told the reporters who woke him the following morning. The Schmidt brothers had been returned to their West Ryde home at about 1.00 a.m., and a bleary-eyed Wolfgang was photographed in his pyjamas as he spoke to the press later that morning. The *Sun*'s 27 January headline? 'WOLFGANG ON THE TRAIL OF A KILLER'

The seventeen-year-old youth brought into the line-up by police was Frank Flanagan of Coogee, who was questioned for five hours before being released. Flanagan's bloodstained jeans were found on Coogee Beach five days earlier and after investigating the matter, detectives were waiting for him when he came home from work that night. It turned out that Flanagan had a simple explanation for the mix-up, which he recounted to reporters who snapped his photograph as he left the police station. The *Daily Mirror* reported Flanagan's comments in its 27 January edition:

> *I cut my leg in an accident four weeks ago and the blood*
> *got on my jeans … I told the police I wasn't at Wanda*

Beach on the day of the murders. I'd never been there until a few days later when I went down for a swim then wandered around out of curiosity … I wish the murderer would give himself up. Until he does, other people are going to come under suspicion.

The fifty detectives assigned to the Wanda Beach murder case — one of the largest squads to undertake a murder investigation in New South Wales at the time — worked amid intense media coverage to ensure that the case did not go away. Pat Burgess wrote in the *Sun* on 20 January, 'The eyes of the whole nation are on Sydney's Police Force as the relentless hunt goes on for the knife murderer who ended the lives of two young girls on Wanda Beach'. Police kept watch on the beach in the days following the murders, with a number of police men and women working undercover dressed as bathers. On Friday, 22 January, NSW Police Commissioner Norm Allen made a public appeal for help. In a statement that took up most of the *Sun*'s front page, Allen expressed his belief that persons in the community held important information that would help solve the Wanda Beach murders:

It is now more than ten days since the young girls Christine Sharrock and Marianne Schmidt were murdered at Wanda Beach, near Cronulla. It is public knowledge that this department is engaged in an all-out investigation to establish the identity of the person or persons responsible for this shocking crime.

I have on more than one occasion asked the public to assist in every way within their powers with information which might help detectives engaged with the case. I now make a further and equally sincere appeal.

I do this because I am satisfied that there must be some

persons in the community who would have some information that they have not brought to the notice of the police.

I put any appeal as high as this — there is a public responsibility to help because there is in our community, a dangerous killer who could strike again.

On Monday, 25 January, the *Daily Mirror* trumpeted, 'The Wanda killer will not be able to hide his identity much longer', but by the end of the month, other events pushed the Wanda Beach investigation off the front page of the newspapers. On 21 January, Lyndon Johnson was inaugurated as the 36th President of the United States; on 26 January, having suffered a stroke ten days before, Sir Winston Churchill slowly slipped into history, aged ninety; closer to home, in a political scandal that shocked Sydney, Ray Septimus Maher, the 53-year-old Speaker of the House in State Parliament, resigned amid allegations of exposing himself to a young typist — the crown defender in that case, John B Kerr, QC, was the future Governor-General of Australia who would write his own place in Australian history when he sacked the Whitlam Government in November 1975.

The press lost its initial fascination with the Wanda Beach murder investigation, except for one small item that provided a sharp sting in the tale. On 21 February 1965 the *Sun* revealed that a £20,000 damages claim that had been made on Marianne's Schmidt's behalf following a car accident in May 1964 had lapsed with her death. Marianne was seriously injured in the accident and admitted to Ryde District Hospital with a fractured skull. Mrs Schmidt had lodged the claim on her daughter's behalf against the driver of the car that hit her, and Solicitor HAP Vernon confirmed that a Supreme Court summons was issued for a nominal amount of £20,000, with the case to be heard in early 1965. As Marianne died before the case began, the claim was automatically voided.

At a time when the median price of a suburban Sydney house was less than £5000, the insurance money would not only have secured the Schmidt family a home, but also Marianne's future education.

Although more than half a century has passed since the Wanda beach murders, both the horrific facts of the case and the many theories about who may have murdered Christine Sharrock and Marianne Schmidt have constantly provided grist for the media mill.

CHAPTER 6
PERSONAL PIECES OF THE PUZZLE

'I bear no malice to[ward] the killer. My little girl has gone to a new life. The killer has still to face his existence in this world. He will be hunted and haunted by the memory.'

Elizabeth Schmidt, the day after the body of her daughter was found buried at Wanda Beach[1]

While each of the Schmidt children provided detectives with important pieces of information about the final movements of Christine and Marianne that furthered the investigation, some details proved to be flawed and contradictory. Detectives were dealing with the fragile minds of young children who were traumatised by the events of 11 January 1965 and struggling to come to terms with the demands placed on them. In re-creating that final trip to the beach, each child's account provides a different perspective of the possible final movements of the two girls.

After the death of his father, sixteen-year-old Helmut Schmidt saw himself as the head of his family. Helmut was not present during Christine and Marianne's New Year's Day visit to Cronulla Beach, nor was he part of the group that went to the beach the day they disappeared; he did, however, accompany Marianne and the children to Cronulla Beach on 2 January, so was able to recount their movements on this day.

On the morning of 2 January, all seven Schmidt children travelled by train to Cronulla for an outing to the beach. When they arrived at around 10.30 a.m. they split into two groups — Trixie, Norbert and Marianne swam in the surf at Cronulla while the other boys went to the southern end of the beach to spear fish off the rocks with the simple equipment Helmut and Hans had brought with them. At about 1.00 p.m., after the group rejoined for lunch, Helmut and Marianne began a conversation with a youth who was watching them in the water. The youth told them he was a police cadet from Queensland and was (according to Hans's description) about seventeen years old, 5 feet 10 inches tall, with a medium build (about 10 stone), fair complexion, round face and short, curly lightbrown hair. The boy smoked Rothmans cigarettes and wore either dark blue or white nylon Speedo-style swimming trunks.

The cadet told the Schmidts about many aspects of his life — he moved from Brisbane to Sydney three or four months earlier; carried out his cadetship at the Police Training Centre in Bourke Street, Redfern; lived in the Regents Park area; worked at a used-car yard in his spare time; and was interested in learning to spear fish because he had fished previously.

At about 12.30 p.m., as Peter and Wolfgang went for a swim at North Cronulla, Marianne went for a walk to Wanda Beach, returning a short time later. She went for another walk at around 2.00 p.m. while Helmut and the cadet were swimming at Cronulla. When Peter and Wolfgang returned from their swim, Helmut asked Wolfgang where she was; Wolfgang replied 'Oh, somewhere up there' and pointed in the direction of Wanda Beach. Marianne had not returned by the time Helmut and the cadet went to the dressing pavilion to change out of their swimming costumes; the cadet put on a pair of jeans but had no shirt or shoes. The cadet left the beach shortly after, at approximately 3.15 p.m.

A short time later — around 3.30 p.m. — Marianne returned, as did Peter and Wolfgang, and the Schmidts reformed their original group. Marianne told her siblings she had been sunbathing and was now sunburnt on her back and neck. At the time Marianne did not say where she had been, but nor was she asked. She did not mention any person she had met along the beach, and Helmut later stated to investigating detectives that he did not see his sister speak to any boy (other than the cadet) that day.

The identity of the cadet who had spoken with the Schmidt children at Cronulla Beach on 2 January was never fully resolved to the satisfaction of investigating police. Interestingly, fourteen years later, police interviewed a 32-year-old Queensland man who was living in Sydney in January 1965 regarding the murders, but nothing came of it.

As the bodies of the two girls were being examined in the Wanda sandhills on 12 January, police took statements from the younger Schmidt children in their home. At this stage the police had not identified the bodies and did not tell the Schmidt children about the discovery. Peter Schmidt, aged ten, confirmed that the group had left their home for the beach at about 8.30 on the previous morning. Peter was the oldest male of the group that went to Wanda Beach on the day the girls died and his statement was succinct and direct:

> *We got the train to Cronulla and we went down to the beach, but it was closed. We had lunch there and Marianne said something about going for a walk to Wanda. We walked along the beach to the last set of flags. The wind was blowing the sand at us and the sand stung our legs and we walked behind a couple of sandhills. Marianne and Christine told us to wait there as they were going back to get the bags, which they had left on the rocks*

on the beach. I watched Marianne and Christine walk over the little sandhill but they didn't walk back to where we had left the bags … they walked the other way. I didn't see the girls with any boys nor did I see them talking to any boys. The girls didn't come back and after about ten minutes I told Wolfgang to go and look for them. He went away and came back within five minutes and I asked him did he see the girls and I can't remember what he told me. That was between 1.00 and 1.30 p.m. We waited for the girls for a long time but they didn't come back so we went back to the rocks where our bags were but the girls were not there. Trixie and Norbert waited there with the bags and Wolfgang and I went back along the beach looking for the girls but we could not find them. We waited there until 5.00 p.m. and the girls didn't come back. I mean by that that we waited on the beach and when they didn't come back we decided we would go home. We then went to the Cronulla railway station and we caught a train, which left just before six o'clock. I took all the children home and [when] we got home I told Hans what had happened.

Peter then added the important, extra information that led police to form a description of the chief suspect:

This morning, Wolfgang told me that yesterday afternoon when he went looking for Marianne and Christine, he saw a boy aged about fourteen … walking along the beach and this boy was in between the two girls.

Wolfgang Schmidt was only seven years old at the time of his sister's death. His statement lacked the cognition of his older brother Peter's and his account was both ambiguous and simplistic, but offered seemingly vital information about the girls' actions prior to their deaths, not least of which was his claim to have seen the above-mentioned boy return from the sandhills alone. In his first interview Wolfgang stated:

Marianne and Christine then went for a walk towards some sandhills. I saw Marianne and Christine then meet a boy and he walked along with them. I followed them and they walked towards the end of the beach. The boy that was walking with Christine and Marianne was walking between them. I then fell over as I was running to catch up with them. When I got up I saw that they had walked into the sandhills. I did not see Marianne and Christine anymore.

A while later, I saw the boy that had walked into the sandhills with Christine and Marianne. He was alone and was walking back down the beach towards me. I said, 'Where are the girls?'. He did not answer me. He then walked away and I did not see him again.

The following day, Wolfgang was interviewed again and described the boy as about sixteen years old:

… like he was going to high school. He was fat and had a lot of light-coloured hair all over his head. I remember that he had some white stuff on his nose. He had long grey trousers on and was carrying a blue towel over his shoulder … [He had] no shirt and no shoes. He was brown. He had cream on his nose. He had hair down each side of his face and on his chin.

Trixie Schmidt, aged nine, also gave a brief statement to police on the night of 12 January and a more detailed account on 10 March. Although her two accounts vary, showing the inaccuracy of children's memories, her statements reveal her to be a bright, attentive young girl. In her initial account, Trixie stated that while at Wanda Beach the previous day her brother Peter had gone to look for Christine and Marianne and had seen two boys playing in the sandhills. 'Wolf also went', she said, 'and he told me that he saw Marianne and Christine walking and there was a boy walking in between them. I did not see any boys myself.'

Two months later, on 10 March, Trixie gave detectives the following account:

On Saturday, January 9, my sister Marianne told me that she was going to take me and Peter, Norbert, Wolf and her friend Christine Sharrock to the beach but we couldn't go on the Sunday because it was raining. She told me that she would take me on the following Monday if it wasn't raining.

On Sunday I went to the Lutheran Church at Town Hall with Helmut, Hans, Peter, Wolf and Norbert and my sister, Marianne. We went to Church in the morning. When we arrived home Marianne prepared our dinner, as Mummy was in hospital. We all stayed at home on the Sunday afternoon and we watched television. We did not have any visitors at my home on the Sunday night.

Early on Monday, January 11, 1965, after we got out of bed, my sister told me that she and Christine were going to take us to the beach at Cronulla. Marianne then made up some sandwiches … and she put some cold water in a thermos flask for us to take to the beach. Christine came into our house and she had a thermos flask too and she had a lime drink in the flask. We had all arranged to go to the beach, with the exception of Helmut and Hans. On the Sunday night Hans said to Marianne that he wanted to go to the beach but she said to him, 'No Hans. We'll be all right'. Hans is thirteen years old.

My brother Helmut was asleep when we left my house on that morning. Hans was in his bedroom when we left and we didn't say goodbye to him. We all had changed into our swimming costumes at my house before we left home and we were wearing our clothes over the costumes. Marianne carried our lunches, our towels and the thermos flask and Christine brought her bag and a towel and she carried them.

Trixie recalled that the group walked to West Ryde railway station, where Marianne bought tickets, and they caught a train to Redfern. While on the train, a tall fifteen-year-old boy talked to Christine and Marianne but Trixie could not hear the subject of their conversation. When the train stopped at Redfern, Christine and the Schmidts exited and the boy stayed on the train. The group went to another platform and waited for their connecting train. Trixie stated that no person spoke to the children on the train to Cronulla.

When the group arrived at Cronulla, the beach was closed, so they walked to the rocks at the southern end of the pool. Trixie remembered:

Wolf wanted to go for a swim but he couldn't because it was too dangerous. Wolf asked again to go for a swim and Marianne still said no. Then Marianne said that she would take him … to the beach and they went in the water. We didn't watch them and we stayed near the rocks and Christine, Norbert, Peter and I went for a paddle in a rock pool.

When Marianne and Wolfgang returned from their swim, the group ate lunch on the rocks (Trixie could not remember

if Christine ate anything) and Marianne then suggested they
go for a walk up to the sandhills:

> *We all walked together towards the sandhills, on the
> beach, and after we had been walking for a long time,
> and after we went up past the houses, the sand was
> hitting us on the legs and the wind was blowing.
> Wolfgang went and left us and then came back and told
> us he had found a place where the sand wouldn't hit us
> so we all went with him to a place in the sand over the
> hill and the sand wasn't blowing there so we all sat down.*
>
> *Marianne and Christine didn't sit down [with us]
> and they put all the towels that we had around us and
> said that they would go on further. Marianne said this.
> I said to Marianne and Christine, 'Where are you
> going?'. Then they said, both of them, to me, 'We're going
> mad'. They didn't say anything else.*
>
> *They walked off together towards the sandhills. They
> walked up a little sandhill and then I couldn't see them
> any more. Peter said to me a while later, I don't know
> how long, 'You go and see if they are coming'. I got up
> and walked up the little sandhill but I could not see
> anyone. We waited a little longer and then Peter told
> Wolfgang to go and have a look, and then Wolfgang
> walked away for a little while then he came back and he
> didn't say anything.*
>
> *We were all sitting with our backs to the water and
> then I saw two boys walking from near the top of the
> sandhills towards the rocks and they were a long way
> away from us. I could see that they both had black hair,
> one boy had a red shirt and the other one had the same.
> I don't know how old they were.*

Although police may have spoken with Norbert Schmidt,
they did not take a statement from him. The youngest of the

Schmidt children, he was just five years old at the time.

On the morning of Wednesday, 13 January, detectives took Peter, Trixie and Wolfgang Schmidt over the same course the children had followed to Cronulla Beach two days earlier. The children, who still did not know of their sister's death, indicated a location about halfway along Wanda Beach as the spot where Christine and Marianne had left them to shelter from the wind while the girls returned to Cronulla to retrieve the beach bags. Wolfgang indicated to the police where he saw the two girls walking in a northerly direction with the chief suspect.

That afternoon at 4.30 doctors allowed Mrs Schmidt to leave hospital and return home for three hours to inform her children of their sister's death. She began by asking Peter, Trixie, Wolfgang and Norbert if they knew what had happened to Christine and Marianne.

'We just lose [*sic*] the girls', came their innocent replies.

Detective Sergeant Keith Paull interviewed Mrs Schmidt that afternoon. He then checked the contents of Marianne's room and took possession of the bag she had taken to the beach the day she died; it contained two return rail tickets, a pair of thongs, a pair of shorts and a watch. Mrs Schmidt confirmed that none of her daughter's property was missing and Helmut confirmed that when the children brought Marianne's beach bag home on 11 January, the towel was wet but the rest of the contents, including her shorts, were dry (the thermos was broken in the bottom of the bag).

Paull also found a number of random rail and bus tickets among Marianne's possessions. Did these tickets belong to someone who accompanied the girls to Cronulla on New Year's Day, or someone they met on the beach? Paull also took possession of Marianne's diary, in case it held the name of a person they planned to meet on the beach that day.

That day, Detectives Sergeants Lawler, Shaw and Brown went to Brush Road to interview Wolfgang Schmidt with a view of building an identikit composite of the boy he saw with Christine and Marianne. The detectives used Wolfgang's description to create a composite picture, but after producing two or three drawings it was noted that the young boy was agreeing with every face put before him.

The detectives then sought Helmut's help in impressing upon Wolfgang the importance of the likeness being produced from his description. With instruction from the detectives, Helmut began to help his younger brother produce another composite but after a while it became clear that Helmut was inadvertently putting his own ideas into Wolfgang's head. When the composite was completed, Helmut turned to the detectives and asked incredulously, 'Do you think that it looks like me?'. By this time, Wolfgang had become uninterested in the process so the detectives decided to make another attempt after a lunch break.

During the break, taken in the lounge room of the Schmidt house, Helmut showed the detectives two letters in Marianne's handwriting; one was torn into small pieces and the other was intact. They were later described by detectives as 'romantic' letters and referred to a boy who went to Marsden High School. The letters were forwarded by Detective Shaw to Cronulla police station for further investigation — in the early stages of the investigation police were working on the theory that the girls knew their killer, but these letters did not shed any light on potential suspects.

After lunch the detectives went to a bedroom at the rear of the house with the four older Schmidt boys where they again attempted to obtain an Identikit composite drawing of the suspect from Wolfgang. According to the official police record, while they were all present, Helmut produced three knives from among his belongings: two were sheath knives and the third was a fishing knife with a serrated edge. Helmut showed each knife, in turn, to the detectives, saying: 'The sheaf [*sic*] knives would not have been the type used to commit the murders but this one [indicating the fishing knife] would have been the type used to commit the murders.'

Could Helmut Schmidt be a suspect in the crime? It would not be the first time someone had been accused of fratricide, and in murder investigations any person can be considered a suspect, from the person who finds the body right back to members of the victim's family. Helmut Schmidt was a naïve teenager, a 'new Australian' dealing with a personal tragedy and rigid police procedure and it is difficult to determine how he should have been expected to behave. Though he did not make a very good impression with these detectives, Helmut was quickly eliminated as a suspect.

The detectives soon abandoned the idea of building up a composite picture of the suspect; the official police report described Wolfgang as 'inattentive and disinterested in the job at hand'.

As the Schmidt household did not have a telephone, the detectives went next door to the Taig residence to call their colleagues and report their failure to build up the composite picture as well as other information they had discovered. They introduced themselves to the Taigs, explaining that they wished to use their telephone to convey information to the police. Detective Sergeant Fred Shaw's 13 January report gave the following account of the conversation:

We found that we were greeted with open hostility by every person in that household. They eventually agreed to allow us to use the phone and after conveying whatever information we had, we left the premises as quickly as possible. It appeared to us at the time that there was

*animosity between the two families, especially the
Sharrock people, who seemed set against the Schmidt
family.*

Detective Sergeant Brown's summary of the interview with
the Schmidt children was also less than flattering:

*At all times during our interview, Wolfgang seemed
especially at a loss as to what was required from him and
was very vague and inattentive to the task placed before
him. Helmut, on the other hand, was light-hearted
about the whole affair, showed no ... noticeable grief,
was ever willing to assist Wolfgang and even went as far
as to place his (Helmut's) interpretations of the suspect
into Wolfgang's head to achieve his own ideas on what
the suspect would look like, or in other words, definitely
romanced about the whole affair throughout.*

The following day, 14 January 1965, Detective Sergeant
Paull visited the Taig family and ascertained that Mrs Taig
had no knowledge of the girls meeting anyone at Wanda or
Cronulla beaches, and that all the articles of clothing
Christine had taken with her, apart from those found on her
body, were accounted for. When told of the cabbage and
celery found in Christine's stomach, Mrs Taig reiterated that
her granddaughter had not taken any prepared food with her
to the beach, only a thermos of limegreen cordial. She had a
£1 note with her and a check of her beach bag revealed the
sum of 5s/4d (54 cents) was left in her purse — Mrs Taig
suggested that Christine could have spent it on food. When
Mrs Taig was informed that a small amount of alcohol was
found in Christine's body, she was shocked and amazed; she
was adamant that Christine 'would not willingly take
alcohol'. When leaving the Taig home, Paull also took a

diary from Christine's room.

The following day, 14 January, Helmut Schmidt was interviewed by police in relation to a railway ticket found in Marianne's beach bag. He could not account for the fact that the railway ticket was dated 3 January and issued at the Narwee railway station for travel between the southern Sydney suburb and the city up to and including 10 January, but revealed that the younger children were in the habit of saving old rail tickets and suggested this was probably where it came from. Inquiries at Narwee station, some 12 kilometres northwest of Wanda Beach, revealed that the stationmaster issued the ticket on Sunday, 3 January — one of 550 adult fares given out that weekend.

On 16 January Detective Sergeants Paull and Shaw interviewed Wolfgang and Trixie Schmidt. The pair stated that while sitting on the rocks at the southern end of Cronulla Beach on 11 January they saw a youth, aged about sixteen with very fair hair, carrying a knife and hunting for crabs. Wolfgang told police he later saw the boy walking south around the rocks where the Schmidt children had been sitting. Wolfgang was adamant that this was the same boy he saw walking with Christine and Marianne at Wanda Beach later that day. This was the first time this connection was made known to police and they quickly requested through newspapers for the 'boy who was seeking crabs to contact Cronulla Police'.

Detective Sergeant Keith Paull's report of 6 February 1965 indicates that in the month following the girls' deaths senior detectives working on the case had formed the opinion that it was:

now … clear that Christine Sharrock and Marianne Schmidt could have directly misled the children into believing that they intended returning from Wanda Beach to the beach at South Cronulla to collect the bags when in fact it was their purpose to walk north along Wanda Beach, knowing that the children would be waiting for them on their return.

Detective Bob Walton interviewed Helmut, Wolfgang and Peter Schmidt on 10 February to follow up this line of inquiry and ascertain whether the girls could have arranged to meet somebody while on their walk. Peter could not remember the girls talking to anyone on the train to Redfern station or on the way to Cronulla. Peter told police that he and the other children had never been to Wanda Beach before and were surprised when Marianne suggested they go for a walk up into the sandhills. In this interview, Peter mentioned for the first time having seen 'two boys with red shirts' sliding down sandhills — the boys Trixie said she had seen while waiting for Christine and Marianne to return. Peter recalled that:

one of these boys was about fifteen and had short white hair, you might call it blond. His hair didn't seem too long, just ordinary cut. He was wearing a red shirt, which had short sleeves. I think he had a grey pair of shorts on … no shoes. The other boy was about fifteen, slightly shorter than the one with the white hair and he could have been thinner. He had black hair. Both boys were carrying airways bags … one of the bags was blue. These boys only stayed there for a short while after the girls had left, and they walked off over the sandhills [indicating a northwesterly direction].

Wolfgang also stated that neither Christine nor Marianne spoke to anyone on either train on the way to Cronulla. The little boy also remembered the games he and Marianne played when they went for a swim and the fact that they did not speak to another person while they were away from the rest of the group on the beach. During this 10 February interview Wolfgang mentioned that while he was eating his lunch he saw a boy 'catching crabs':

The boy that was catching crabs had a knife. He was holding it in his hand. He didn't have it in his hand all the time. I can't explain it right now. He had the knife in a holster like Helmut's all the time. He didn't have the knife in his hand at all. He had the long thing in his hands. It had a point. We have something like it at home [a spear]. It goes with a spear gun and is about this long [indicating a length of about three feet]. He had it in one hand and he was trying to get a crab out of the crack.

Wolfgang maintained that Christine and Marianne spoke to this boy catching crabs on the rocks, and that it was a little after this that they decided to walk to Wanda Beach, although the girls never mentioned wanting to be at a particular place by a specific time. Wolfgang told detectives that when the girls left the children in the sandhills, he merely thought that the girls wanted to walk up the sandhills before going home. As the children waited for Christine and Marianne to return, Wolfgang walked up into the sandhills and 'saw that boy again. I am sure of this. I saw him again with the girls in the sandhills. I heard him speaking to the girls. Peter told me to look for them and I saw them with the boy.'

'They were this far away', Wolfgang said, indicating a distance of about ten yards before continuing:

He said to the girls, 'What's your name?' The girls didn't say anything to him. The boy looked angry. I say he looked angry because his face looked angry. The boy was walking on the sandhills between Christine and Marianne. I was walking in front of them and to their left.

Wolfgang then demonstrated what he meant and it was consistent with his being able to see the boy's face. 'I didn't walk far with them. Christine and Marianne and this boy were not laughing and joking as they walked along.'

Wolfgang described the boy as approximately sixteen years old, with hair 'the same colour as Christine': this would make the boy's hair light brown, not blond as was reported in the media from day one. Wolfgang continued:

It was combed back … blowing about in the wind that day because it was greasy. He had long grey pants on and nothing else and his [royal blue] towel was over his right shoulder … He hadn't started to shave yet. He had cream on his nose. I would know him again by his face …

When he was up on the sandhills when I saw him talking to the girls, his knife was in the holster. He didn't have the spear. When he came back along the beach afterwards, he still had the holster on but there was no knife in it. I said to him, 'Where are the girls?' and he didn't say anything and he was shaking a little bit.

Wolfgang's story seemed to be more embellished each time he told it, so Mrs Schmidt sought to clarify certain points by talking to her son in his native German. 'He always says the boy he saw was dressed the same', she told the police. 'He always says it was the boy he saw on the rocks.' As to the young boy's credibility, Mrs Schmidt was adamant: 'I believe Wolfgang because he always says the same thing'.

Detectives Walton, Johnson and Aitken later took Mrs

Schmidt, Peter and Wolfgang to Cronulla Beach, where Mrs Schmidt indicated the position on the rocks where she and her husband used to picnic with their family before his death: the position was easily identifiable because it had the letter 'M' scratched into the rock wall. Wolfgang and Peter then led the detectives south around the rocks and both boys (separately) identified the place the group had eaten lunch on the day of the murders. They also identified the ledge where Christine and Marianne had left the beach bags when they went for their fatal walk to Wanda.

Wolfgang indicated a pool of water in the rocks where the unidentified youth had been hunting crabs. When asked where the crab the boy had caught was, Wolfgang ran over to a small ledge of rock and answered, 'He caught that naughty crab there'. After the boys had left the area, one of the detectives lifted up the ledge of rock and found a number of crabs underneath it.

The police now considered a new scenario:[2] had the girls befriended someone — a youth — on the beach that day and, if not exactly arranging to meet him later, been stalked by the youth on their way to the sandhills? Could the youth have charmed the girls into sharing a meal with him … a Chinese meal? On a sandhill? This appears unlikely. Perhaps it was a spring roll, a popular deep-fried vegetable snack that you could hold in your hand as you ate it. But the alcohol? Would Christine have drunk some of the murderer's beer? Unlikely, according to Mrs Taig. Perhaps Christine simply ate cucumber sandwiches and some fruit, which then fermented in her stomach.

By the end of February the police were desperate for a breakthrough in the investigation, and the strongest lead remained the youth seen hunting crabs and who was allegedly seen walking with the girls before they died. At 8.00 a.m. on 28 February — seven weeks after the murders

— Detectives Walton and Aitken took Wolfgang Schmidt to the Narwee railway station to see if the young boy could identify the suspect. From 8.00 a.m. to 1.00 p.m., Wolfgang, the two detectives and a local railway patrolman watched every person on the platform; could the Narwee–City ticket that Marianne Schmidt souvenired on the day she died be the key to solving the crime? The group waited all day but did not see anybody matching the youth's description.

Keith Paull, now long retired, explained in an interview for this book (in September 2002) the problems police had with the young boy's account of what happened on the day the girls died:

We didn't know nor could we establish one way or another whether, as happens with young children sometimes, they got carried away with the line of a particular conversation. An adult says, 'Did you see the girls with anybody?' and children are not always as accurate as you might think. I'm in no way trying to detract from anything the boy might have said except to say that being a child, we couldn't believe 100 per cent of what he was saying as being correct.

Paull commented that the Schmidt children 'were as helpful as one could expect … what we were looking for was corroboration with the other children's stories'. This corroboration could not be found; none of the other Schmidt children saw the two girls with the suspect, and the police may well have exerted a lot of time and manpower looking for a suspect who may not even have existed.

As early as February 1965, the police investigation was grinding to a standstill.

CHAPTER 7

THE POLICE INVESTIGATION

'This [crime] appears to be an insane, sadistic killing rather than a sex crime. I believe the murderer is a schizophrenic — a late teenager or in his early twenties … withdrawn, unsociable, peculiar in his mannerisms. The sexual side of the crime is secondary. The killer is young, cunning and given to sudden violence. (He is) suffering a grave, mental disturbance.'

Dr John McGeorge, a leading forensic psychiatrist, January 1965[1]

The announcement of a record £10,000 reward for information leading to the arrest of the Wanda Beach murderer flooded the NSW Police with a mountain of paperwork and a multitude of erroneous reports. Not only was every blond-haired, sixteen year-old 'surfie-type' now a potential suspect — following Wolfgang Schmidt's vague description — but the reward also flushed out the garrulous, the greedy and the insane. Some rang anonymously, some under the influence of alcohol and some with an axe to grind. 'Yes, my husband has been acting suspiciously', a female voice would say on the end of the line. 'He'll be home from the pub at nine o'clock if you want to come and question him.'

As a result, police questioned many people who turned out to have no connection with the crime. A stowaway found aboard a freighter bound for England was even questioned about the murders — the freighter left Sydney within thirty-six hours of the murders and the captain immediately contacted Sydney detectives when the stowaway was found; the young man was later cleared. A shirtless youth seen at Cronulla railway station on the night of the murders was investigated; two youths in Newcastle were questioned and released; while interviews with an eighteen-year-old Merrylands man came to naught. Police investigated a man who was staying at the Wanda Surf Club residence — the eighteen-year-old, fair-haired youth was holidaying from Queensland and had arrived at Wanda Beach on the afternoon of the murders; a quick check found he had no involvement in the crime.

Some of the calls to police contained only the slightest relation to the investigation … An anonymous caller stated that at 9 p.m. on the night of 11 January 1965 he saw a red Holden sedan containing a number of youths and two girls travelling in an easterly direction along Parraweena Road, in the Sutherland suburb of Caringbah … A man called police to say he had noticed that a young man who worked at a local newsagency matched the general description of the sixteen-year-old, blond-haired suspect … 'Police Running Sheet 49' was simply headed 'UNKEPT [*sic*] SURFIE TYPE YOUTH SEEN AT BEACON'S HILL ON 13.1.65' … A truck driver even rang police twice to inform them that Christine Sharrock had once served him at Anthony Horden's department store.

Every report was investigated and, although most were a waste of police time and resources, some had a ring of intrigue about them and required more detailed investigation. A Caringbah man reported that on the day after the bodies were found he was picnicking with his young family and next-door neighbour at the Woronora

Weir, off Heathcote Road on the southern outskirts of Sydney, not far from the Cronulla area. At 11.00 a.m. he helped a young man retrieve keys he had locked inside his battered, cream-coloured 1954 Holden sedan. The youth was about twenty years old, 5 feet 7 inches tall with dark hair and a 'smallish head with lean features, slightly stooped'. As the keys were recovered from his locked car, the young man said, unsolicited, 'You know those girls murdered at Cronulla? I think I know who did it. He was a chap like me with long black hair.' A year later, the body of a Sydney prostitute was found nearby on the Old Illawarra Road (see Chapter 10); she had been mutilated in a similar manner to Christine Sharrock and Marianne Schmidt. Had this Caringbah family stumbled upon a serial killer staking out his territory? Police were unable to track down the man or his car.

Standard police procedure in discounting potential suspects begins with considering the person or persons who report the crime, as well as investigating each eyewitness account and interviewing known associates of the victims, including their families. Police were quickly able to eliminate as suspects Peter Smith, who discovered the bodies; Dennis Dostine, who gave one of the most important accounts of the final movements of the girls; Barry Ezzy, the lifeguard on duty the day the girls were murdered and the day their bodies were discovered; and every other person on the beach that day who came forward with information.

With no suspect known to them, police continued to follow many lines of inquiry after the murders disappeared from the front pages of the newspapers. The only report of property being stolen on the day the girls were murdered was at nearby Cronulla Beach. A Gymea woman reported that her fourteen-year-old son's blue jeans, silver-buckled black leather belt and long-sleeved brown-and-orange-striped shirt were taken from the sand, but the clothing belonging to his friend (left in the same place) remained untouched, although a £10 note was stolen. Conjectures could be made: the killer would have been covered by blood; he may even have been nude: what better way to escape than to have a spare pair of clothes secreted in the sand dunes?

The day the girls' bodies were discovered, a Cronulla man found a pair of black flippers by the water's edge half a mile north of Wanda Beach. Another scenario: had the killer swum unnoticed to Wanda Beach and laid in wait for his victims? When a crudely made crab spear — the metal spear tip tied to a piece of wood, possibly part of a fence post — was found washed up on that part of the beach, detectives tried to link it to the youth the Schmidt children had encountered hunting crabs at the southern end of the beach. The problem was that the spear looked like any number of makeshift spears locals used to hunt crabs — even the older Schmidt boys had one like it.

Detectives also explored the theory that the girls were murdered by someone who frequented the sandhills at Wanda Beach and was lying in wait for a victim, any victim. Of particular concern was the number of suspects the sandhills revealed. In a September 2002 interview for this book, former Detective Sergeant Keith Paull recalled:

The more we investigated the case, and I was there for eleven months, the more homosexuals, suspected perverts and people, shall we say with 'loose morals', we found who frequented the area not far from where the bodies of the girls were found. Greenhills was a particular haunt for homosexual men and we … interviewed as many of them as possible in regard to whether they could assist us. Put it this way, we interviewed as many as one could identify because a lot of the men who frequented the area for 'homosexual activity' were only known by nicknames and aliases, while many others did not even identify themselves to their partners.

In 1965, Sydney was a conservative society and homosexuality among consenting adults was a criminal act. Topless sunbathing was something of a phenomenon; a social aberration that attracted its fair share of voyeurs. One man investigated for his penchant for nude sunbathing in the sandhills at Wanda was later found to be a respected bank manager working in a nearby suburb who had found a novel way of spending his afternoons. Once the investigating police had checked Christine and Marianne's backgrounds it became obvious that the girls did not know they were walking into a potential minefield when they left the younger Schmidt children in the sandhills and began their fateful walk to Greenhills. 'There was some conjecture that someone on the beach had asked them to go for a walk up there … It was a very tense time', said lifeguard Barry Ezzy when interviewed for this book in October 2002. A long-time Cronulla resident, Ezzy added: 'Nothing like this had happened before. There was a lot of speculation as to who might have done it'.

In the weeks following the murders Ezzy grew to recognise the undercover police men and women posing as bathers on the beach in the hope of catching the murderer returning to the scene of the crime. Ezzy knew the area was a well-known haunt for what he termed 'poofters and perverts': 'When you went for a run over the dunes or a walk along the beach, heads would be popping up like gophers.'

Every serial pest who set foot on the Cronulla beachhead was brought to the attention of the investigating police.

Shirley Lennon (not her real name) reported one such pest, who became a significant person of interest to the police. Mrs Lennon was in the habit of sunbathing in the sandhills south of Wanda Surf Club at the small, unpatrolled Elouera Beach during the summer months from November 1963 to January 1965. She provided police with a detailed description of the 'serial pest': approximately 5 feet 11 inches tall; with dark brown–almost black hair brushed to one side; brown eyes; a round, chubby face that looked 'very babyish'; weighing about 12 stone but not of a solid build — 'more like flabby fat' were Mrs Lennon's words. The man was wearing long grey trousers and a Bonds athletic singlet.

In late November or early December of 1963, Mrs Lennon was sitting on Cronulla Beach, wearing a bikini and applying suntan lotion, when a young man approached her from behind, coming from the direction of Wanda Beach. There was nobody else in the area at the time and when the man asked Mrs Lennon if she would mind his towel while he went for a swim, she told him to leave it there and she would keep an eye on it. To her surprise, the man laid out his towel right next to hers and sat down on it.

The man then took a book from his hip pocket and began looking through it. A few minutes later he held the book open so Mrs Lennon could see it and said, 'How big would those tits be?'. Mrs Lennon saw a picture of a big-busted woman; on the opposite page was a picture of a nude woman. She turned her head away and told the man to wake up to himself. The man continued holding the book in front of Mrs Lennon's face, turning over the pages that contained a series of nude women in different poses. He asked Mrs Lennon if she would like to read the book and — ignored her request for him to move away from her.

Mrs Lennon began to grow concerned about the situation,

particularly when the man asked her if she would like him to remove his trousers. 'I have my costume on', he told her, 'and if I open my legs you can see what I've got'.

Mrs Lennon ignored him, refusing to look at him and concentrating on her own magazine. She heard him turning the pages of his book as he continued to make lewd comments to himself. After a while, she lifted her arm as she shifted her weight in the sand and he said: 'That's right. Do that again. I can see your tits. But next time you do it, squeeze yourself together so they will come out more.'

Mrs Lennon was now too frightened to get up and walk away so continued to ignore him and stare at her magazine, refusing to make eye contact with him.

The man then began to ask her vulgar questions, which she refused to answer: 'What size cunt do you have?'; 'Have different size women got different size cunts?'; 'I have never seen what one looks like. Describe it to me'. As Mrs Lennon would explain to police, the man continued talking about female sexual organs until she told him that she was expecting her husband soon and that he'd better leave. She insulted the man a number of times, hoping he would leave, but he ignored her. A few times he got up and walked over into the nearby sandhills but came back over to her and continued his lewd conversation.

Finally Mrs Lennon said: 'My husband will punch you when he comes and I tell him what you have been saying. You'd better go.' The man then left.

After this initial encounter, Mrs Lennon saw the man on numerous occasions, always between Cronulla and Wanda beaches. The man always carried a towel, and sometimes a transistor radio. He occasionally sat beside her and attempted to draw her into a lewd conversation but each time she got up and walked away; other days Mrs Lennon witnessed him walking along the water's edge between Wanda and Cronulla

— always alone.

Detectives investigating the Wanda Beach murders were particularly interested when Mrs Lennon reported that on one occasion the man had approached her and offered to go and get some beer and bring it back for her. Christine Schmidt's autopsy had found a level of alcohol in her body; was this the breakthrough connection the police needed? They added this man to their list of suspects and dubbed him 'The Fat Man'. Mrs Lennon's story gained added credence from the significant number of people who corroborated her description of the beach pest, especially those who saw him in the Wanda Beach area on the day Christine and Marianne were murdered. All the descriptions given by these witnesses were consistent with a police drawing of the serial beach pest and helped police to retrace his movements on the day.

At 10.00 a.m. on 11 January 1965, two young women noticed the suspect standing on the sand near the corner of Mitchell and Bando Roads near the entrance to Elouera Beach. He was carrying a folded newspaper and mumbling to himself as he sat down behind the girls. He later moved over to two other girls on the beach and spoke to them before walking off in the direction of Wanda Beach. The girls waited until the suspect was out of sight before leaving the beach at approximately 10.20 a.m. to return to a flat in a nearby street, where one of them lived. From the flat, which overlooked North Cronulla Beach, the women saw the suspect walk along the grass footpath in Prince Street towards North Cronulla Surf Club at about 11.00 a.m. A short time later, while they sipped tea and looked down onto the beach, they saw him walk back along Prince Street towards Wanda Beach, and between 12.30 p.m. and 1.30 p.m. the women saw him make one last trip along Prince Street southwards and then walk back towards Wanda Beach.

The same morning, a sixteen-year-old Bankstown girl was at Elouera Beach and noticed the suspect standing near the water's edge. She also noted that he was carrying a rolled newspaper and a transistor radio — had the murderer, whoever he was, concealed a knife in a rolled up newspaper as he searched for a victim?

The suspect turned around and when he saw the teenager on the beach came within two feet of her and spoke. 'Hello, I'm from Adelaide', the man said. 'Are there any good beaches around here?' The girl ignored the ridiculousness of the question — they were on a beach at the time — and said no. The man sat down beside her for about ten minutes and attempted to strike up a conversation with her. She heard the twelve o'clock pips sound on the man's radio and was then amazed to hear him ask her what the time was — she told him the pips on the radio indicated that it was twelve o'clock.

'I come from Adelaide', the man said again. 'I'm on holidays. How about the sex in Sydney? All these girls walk around in these bikinis. They are that small you would think they would hurt them.' The girl ignored the man as he continued to speak to her. 'Do you have a boyfriend?', he asked. 'Where do you live?'

The girl quickly made an excuse to leave and got up and started walking south towards Cronulla Beach. The suspect told her that he too had to go and headed north towards Wanda Beach. The girl estimated the time to be approximately 12.20 p.m. Later that afternoon — about the time Christine and Marianne left the Schmidt children and began their final walk — the girl walked up towards the North Cronulla dressing sheds and noticed the suspect lurking around. He passed within five feet of her and headed north towards Wanda Beach. She did not see him again.

A third sighting of the suspect on the day of the murders was reported by two young women, who were approached by 'The Fat Man' at about 11.00 a.m. as they sat on the grass in front of North Cronulla Surf Club. The suspect told the girls he came from Adelaide and, as previously that day, commented on the beach attire of the girls, saying: 'A lot more girls in Adelaide wear bikinis than they do over here'. He then asked where Wanda Beach was, so they pointed in a northerly direction. The man continued to try to draw the girls into a conversation and asked them if they wanted to look at his pornographic book, at which point they got up and left, noticing that the man walked down onto North Cronulla Beach. The time was now 11.45 a.m.

Approximately fifteen minutes later the suspect approached another pair of young women as they sat on the grass in front of the North Cronulla surf shed. As earlier, the man told these women he was from Adelaide and commented that the girls wearing bikinis 'looked sexy … Look at that girl over there in the bikini. When she moves you can see her privates.'

The man then asked the women if they would like to look at his book of nude girls; as with the other witnesses, the women got up and walked away. One of the women later identified the man from police drawings as looking like the dark-haired beach pest, except that his hair was very thick and ruffled all over his head.

The final reported sighting of 'The Fat Man' on 11 January was at about 12.10 p.m., when 26-year-old Brian McCann saw the suspect walk over and speak to a girl sitting on the sand at Elouera Beach. McCann described the girl as approximately fifteen years old and the suspect as approximately twenty-four. McCann then saw the suspect approach two girls who were sitting on the water's edge, who got up and moved away. The suspect walked back towards the roadway and stopped to look down over the beach, as if observing the area, then walked diagonally towards the water's edge in a northerly direction. McCann last saw the suspect in front of the Wanda Beach Surf Club, walking north along the beach, at approximately 12.40 p.m. McCann told police he was not sure if the suspect was carrying anything in his hands.

A week after the Wanda Beach murders, Mrs Lennon again contacted local police to report a beach pest — who also became a police suspect — but not 'The Fat Man' who had previously harassed her. In the week following New Year's Day 1965, Mrs Lennon again went to sunbathe in the sandhills between Wanda and Cronulla beaches, where a young man approached her. Mrs Lennon described this man as between eighteen and twenty years old, with a slim build, light brown hair and wearing a longsleeved shirt tucked into a pair of fawn shorts. Mrs Lennon also stated that teeth were missing from the man's upper jaw.

The suspect asked Mrs Lennon how much money she wanted for 'a naughty' and after being told to leave said, 'It's worth fifty quid to you.' When Mrs Lennon did not answer, he said, 'I'll give you a hundred quid then.'

'Do you think I am a prostitute, making a suggestion like that to me?' she replied.

'Well, you're up in the sandhills', the suspect replied. 'Go on, I'd like to see what size cunt you have. I would like to fuck you. You will only be gone five minutes. I have a flat down the street.'

Mrs Lennon berated the man, telling him he made her sick; the suspect then walked away over the sandhills and down towards Girrilang Road, which runs perpendicular to North Cronulla Beach.

Between ten and fifteen minutes later, Mrs Lennon heard a voice behind her, coming up from the beach: 'I've got it, I've got it'. She turned around and saw the young man who had propositioned her earlier: he held out a roll of folded bank notes and said: 'I've brought the money back to you. It's yours for five minutes' work.'

Mrs Lennon again told the man to leave her alone but he grew agitated and excited, saying, 'I've got to have it, I've got to have it … Let me fuck you, it will only take you five minutes. Let me have a look at your cunt'.

At that time a man and young boy walked by; the suspect moved and sat about two yards away, counting his money. When the man and young boy sat down nearby, Mrs Lennon took the opportunity to get up and walk to her car. The suspect then got up and walked in the direction of Wanda Beach.

While it may not have been a giant leap in the public's mind to equate 'pervert' with 'murderer', detectives could only conjecture why a serial beach pest who made himself known to several women over the course of many visits to the beach would one day turn into a rapist and killer.

A third suspect was reported by a park ranger from Caringbah, Robert Bland, and his daughter. On 11 December 1964, a man exposed himself in the sandhills while the young girl was riding her horse. The naked man chased the girl for a short distance and was seen a week later in an undressed state in the sandhills. The man was described as 30–35 years old, between 5 feet 10 inches and 6 feet tall, with black hair balding in the front, solid athletic build, very hairy on the body, very suntanned and of 'foreign' appearance.

Horseriders in the Greenhills area also reported this man; one local woman stated that she saw the man up to a dozen times between September and December and that he was nude on at least eleven occasions. The man appeared to be waiting in the sandhills and when women passed, walked out naked.

This man was thought to be the same suspect observed by a couple at about 1.00 p.m. on 11 January 1965. The husband and wife, trying to escape the windy conditions, sat in their car on Mitchell Road, which ran parallel to the beach, and had an uninterrupted view of the beach all the way up to Kurnell. They saw two young girls walking in the sandhills about fifty yards in front of their vehicle. A number of other small children played near them, about 100 yards in front of the pair and closer to the water. About 2.15 p.m., the couple noticed a man who wore a swimming costume and carried a blue towel walking in a southerly direction from Kurnell. From inside the car, the pair watched the man for about five minutes as he walked along the sandhills about 50 yards in front of their car and 150–200 yards in from the water. The man then walked into the sandhills towards the Wanda Surf Club and disappeared.

On 15 February 1965 an undercover detective who was patrolling Wanda Beach chased a suspect into the sandhills, but the man eluded him. The man was described as 25–30 years old, 5 feet 9 inches tall, with solid build, medium complexion, dark hair (balding) and wearing a red swimming costume. The following day, the same person was seen masturbating in the sandhills and on 17 March that year, a woman and her young brother were walking along Wanda Beach when the same man exposed himself and started to masturbate 300 yards south of the Wanda Surf Club.

Warrants were issued for the arrest of the suspects outlined above but were never served on any known people. Inquiries were also made at all psychiatric hospitals and centres in New South Wales, with numerous interviews taking place but to no avail. Some 5000 suspects were questioned in relation to the murders of Christine Sharrock and Marianne Schmidt but most were quickly determined to have had no connection with the crime. Police suspended inquiries regarding a number of other suspects because no further information was available to continue useful investigations.

On 22 April 1966 the Coroner's findings on the Wanda Beach murders was finally handed down. In his official report, the Stipendiary Magistrate and Sydney City Coroner, JJ Loomes, wrote:

> *These inquiries charge me as Coroner to inquire on the part of our Sovereign Lady the Queen, when and where the deceased Marianne Schmidt and Christine Mary Sharrock came to their deaths and the manner and cause of their deaths.*
>
> *The compass of that charge is contained in the words of Mr Justice Wills to the Grand Jury in the Crew Murder Trial in Chester, England. I quote the relevant extract, 'The Coroner also has one advantage from a certain point of view, namely that being fettered by no precise rules of evidence and bound to collect as far as he could all information which could throw any light on the cause of death, where death had taken place under suspicious circumstances he could often times collect evidence, facts and statements which, whether or not they might ultimately be capable to being turned into evidence against any parties to be put upon trial, were often very valuable as supplying materials for investigations by the police and as affording clues which might lead to successful inquiries.'*
>
> *Evidence has been tendered to this Inquest of the exhaustive police inquiries that have been undertaken in the search for the person or persons responsible for the deaths of the two deceased. The evidence and the magnitude of those inquiries is before this Court, some twenty-one volumes comprising as they do of some 5000 pages and quoting the evidence of Det. Sgt. Douglass, the*

Officer in Charge of the police inquiries, representing interviews with some 7000 people.

There would appear, therefore, only the remotest possibility that at this Inquest some insignificant fact may emerge which could be the key to the mystery — yet strangely there is on record an Inquest which precisely did just that and I refer to what is known as 'The Brides in the Bath' Inquest in England in 1915 where the publicity given to that Inquest led to the detection of the Crime and the ultimate conviction of the murderer.

One of the reasons for an Inquest is to provide an opportunity for public examination of the thoroughness of the Police, Medical and Scientific Investigations and to have the facts brought out into the open. An Inquest is not a finale to the proceedings, it could be just the beginning, for inquiries will go on and continue to go on in an endeavour to find the answer to these deaths.

The Cause of Death is very evident, a vicious, brutal murder. The Crime took place in the vicinity of a Sydney Beach on a summer's day during school holidays and in the middle of the day. That suggests that there must be surely someone who could throw some light on this happening. If there is that someone has not come forward and apparently will not come forward even in the fact of a reward of no less than $20,000, a reward I might add that is still in existence.

It seems strange that although laws are made for the preservation and protection of society there are those who will protect or shield the wrongdoer. Even our own efforts today seem directed more to the rehabilitation of the criminal to the exclusion of the protection of society, and praiseworthy though that may be the protection of society should surely be the first consideration.

I do not intend to canvass the evidence given or to comment on it — to do so can serve no purpose and could perhaps hinder the inquiries that, as I have previously said, are going on and will continue to go on and, after looking at the photographs of the bodies of these two young girls, one is so revolted by the viciousness and callousness of this crime that it can be hoped these inquiries will be even intensified, difficult though that may be.

My findings in respect of the deaths are as follows:

MARIANNE SCHMIDT
I FIND THAT THE DECEASED MARIANNE SCHMIDT ON THE ELEVENTH DAY OF JANUARY, 1965, ON SANDHILLS NORTH OF WANDA BEACH AND KNOWN AS GREENHILLS DIED FROM HAEMORRHAGE THE RESULT OF A CUT THROAT AND FOUR PENETRATING WOUNDS OF THE CHEST INFLICTED UPON HER ON THAT DATE AND AT THAT PLACE.

CHRISTINE MARY SHARROCK
I FIND THAT THE DECEASED CHRISTINE MARY SHARROCK ON THE ELEVENTH DAY OF JANUARY, 1965, ON SANDHILLS NORTH OF WANDA BEACH AND KNOWN AS GREENHILLS DIED FROM HAEMORRHAGE AS THE RESULT OF PENETRATING WOUNDS OF THE CHEST ASSOCIATED WITH INJURIES NAMELY A FRACTURE OF THE SKULL AND INJURY TO THE BRAIN INFLICTED UPON HER ON THAT DATE AND AT THAT PLACE.

Over the next eight years, until the final police résumé of the unsolved crime was concluded in 1973, 14 000 people were interviewed concerning the Wanda Beach murders. The results of these investigations are today contained in eighty-one volumes of police reports containing over 10,000 pages of typed running sheets. In 1966, following the adoption of decimal currency, the record reward offered by the NSW Government for information leading to the conviction of the person/s responsible for the murders of Christine Sharrock and Marianne Schmidt was converted to $20,000. Disappointingly, the reward has remained frozen at this level for almost four decades, but is still in force today.

CHAPTER 8
CHRISTINE AND MARIANNE REMEMBERED

'The subject … is the oldest of four children, residing at the address stated with her parents who exercise <u>very strict</u> control over her activities. She is a very intelligent, although shy and reserved type of girl who attends the convent mentioned in her statement, where she receives religious instruction and teaching from the Catholic Sisters. She is not an associate of any undesirable element and [is] a person of exemplary character.'

Detective Constable Owen's footnote at the bottom of Margaret Kavazos's statement regarding her friendship with Christine Sharrock[1]

Drop a rock into the stillness of an undisturbed lake and in time the ripples will make their way to the shore. The murder of two teenage girls in the sandhills at Wanda Beach affected the girls' families and friends, and indeed the police who investigated the crime, for the remainder of their lives. There were no psychological counselling, victim support groups or criminal impact statements in the 1960s. The pain, grief and guilt felt by those who knew Christine Sharrock and Marianne Schmidt during their short lives, and by those who were privy to the shocking details of their deaths, manifested itself in different ways over the following years.

Margaret Kavazos knew Christine Sharrock longer and more intimately than any other friend. They started kindergarten together at St Therese's Catholic Girls School in Lakemba in the late 1950s and became very close friends from the first day. During interviews for this book,[2] Margaret, now aged sixty-five and a single mother of three grown sons, was able to create a clear picture of the friend she remembered; she had not spoken of her friendship with Christine for many years:

> *We grew up together and shared everything together … We were very ordinary types of girls … we weren't 'party' girls and didn't go out that much. Christine, though, because of her particular circumstances in living with her grandmother in West Ryde, had a little bit more freedom than I did. My parents were very strict. I would never have been allowed to go to the beach by myself, on the train and unsupervised. Ever. But because she was living with her grandmother and because of the number of Schmidt children going that day, her grandmother thought that it would have been safe …*
>
> *Because of her circumstances, she travelled on trains, sometimes at night, where I would never have been allowed to do that. She was streetwise in that regard. She used to travel to Lakemba by train every school day. My mother would walk me to the front gate and watch me get onto the bus outside our house!*

Quite simply, Christine was Margaret's best friend:

> *Christine was a beautiful girl … she was very trusting, and that's why I believe she was killed that day at Wanda*

Beach — because she was so trusting of people. Christine would have implicitly trusted whoever approached the girls on the beach that day.

Living at West Ryde, Christine was isolated from her school friends at Lakemba. 'My dad used to drive me to West Ryde all the time', Margaret recalls. 'I would spend weekends there and Christine would stay at my house at Belfield. There was absolutely nothing to do in West Ryde. It was a very nondescript enclave of war service homes.'

When the Schmidt family moved to Brush Road, Christine found someone her own age she could share things with:

> *That's the sort of person Christine was … Once she made a friend, she became inseparable from them. When Marianne moved next door to her, Christine still included me in a lot of her activities but I was like a third wheel … Christine was a lot closer to Marianne and I had a boyfriend at that stage. I was entering into a totally different life. I wasn't as caught up in the 'boy craziness' as much as Christine and Marianne obviously were. I also grew up with three brothers in my household so I found all the 'boy talk' … I* hope he likes me … *fairly tedious and boring.*

In the first week of January 1965, Christine phoned Margaret and told her about the New Year's Day visit to Cronulla Beach and that she and Marianne and were planning to go again that weekend:

> *Christine wanted me to stay at her place the week she died. I could very easily have been with them that day at Wanda Beach. My family was going away on holidays and I had no choice but to go away with them but I can*

remember putting up a fight and saying that I really wanted to stay with Christine. But there was no way my mother and father were going to leave me behind in Sydney … My parents were adamant, 'We're going on holidays and you're coming with us.'

Margaret was in Brisbane with her family when she heard the terrible news. 'I was given a transistor radio for Christmas and the first thing I did when I hopped out of bed each morning was turn it on.' The news broadcast on the morning of 13 January 1965 identified Christine and Marianne as the two girls found dead at Wanda Beach. Margaret was transfixed: 'I have never really got over the shock of hearing their names … it affected my whole life.'

Margaret recalled the reaction within her immediate family:

My family are good people but none of us knew how to handle the situation … Mum was by my side and was very worried about me. But you had to be stoic and not let it show that it hurt so much. That is how we dealt with grief in those days. My dad couldn't understand why we should pack up the family and return to Sydney for a funeral. It was more out of frustration — we'd just arrived, what were we going to do now? Drive back to Sydney? The feeling was that going to a funeral wasn't going to change anything. Nobody knew what to do. All the adults were at a loss.

I finally took it upon myself to make the decision not to go back for Christine's funeral. The next morning I told my parents that I didn't want to go back … like it was my idea, but I was only trying to do what I thought was the right thing by my parents. Some part of me didn't want to come back to Sydney because then I would have to admit to myself that Christine and Marianne had been murdered. 'As long as I am away I can keep pretending to myself that it isn't real', I told myself …

The other problem was that we didn't know when the funeral was being held.

The bodies of the two girls were not released until a week after their deaths and Margaret's family returned to Sydney just days after Christine's funeral.

Margaret couldn't hide from the blanket media coverage of the murders, even in Brisbane. Her Christmas present, the portable transistor radio that had brought her the grim news, constantly interrupted her peace of mind: 'It was on the radio all the time and on billboards outside newsagencies.' 'THE WANDA BEACH MURDERS' was splashed everywhere.

Police contacted Margaret after her family returned to Sydney — 'The police were obviously working on the angle that the killer may have been someone that we knew and that I might have some information' — but she could not shed any light on possible suspects.

Margaret's parents drove her to the Taig's house to visit Christine's grandparents. It was immensely difficult to go back to Brush Road, but it was something she had to do:

Nan Taig couldn't wait to see me. She needed to keep talking about what happened and to cry it out of her system. I remember Christine's grandfather sitting quietly in his chair. Numbed by the tragedy, he never talked about it.

Nan took me into Christine's room and gave me some of her things to remember her by. Christine had recently bought a new pair of shoes and Nan wanted me to have them. I wasn't sure about it but Nan was adamant. I was wearing them one day when I bumped into Christine's mother at the railway station. I am sure she noticed the shoes first and she looked up and saw that it was me. 'They're just like Christine's shoes', she said. I had to tell her they were Christine's shoes. I felt terrible and she could see that, but she told me she was glad I had them. I always felt incredibly sad for Mrs Maher [Christine's mother]. She was a very gentle woman. After Christine's death she wasn't bitter. I think she had enough guilt of her own to deal with. Christine was hostile to her mother's new marriage and never felt part of her stepfamily. She wanted her mother all to herself or not at all. They were not close when Christine died.

Tragically, Christine's mother, stepfather and stepbrother were away on holidays when she was murdered.

During her visit to the Taig household, Margaret noticed that anger had set in: 'There was definitely tension between the two families. The feeling was [that] Christine would never have gone to the beach in the first place, except for the Schmidt family. Nan never blamed anyone in particular … just criticised.' The fact that the media coverage tended to focus on the Schmidt children added to this hostility. The Schmidt family, in Nan's words, spent 'good money they didn't have' to cosmetically prepare Marianne's body, especially her face, for the funeral.

'Nan thought that was an outrageous waste of money', Margaret says. 'It just wasn't part of our Australian culture. Nan couldn't afford to have that done for Christine, but neither would she ever think of doing it.'

Although Margaret knew Nan Taig's bitterness was unfair, she understood it. Like Christine's grandmother, Margaret could also not help thinking at the time that if the Schmidts had not moved next door to the Taigs, her friend might still be alive:

> *I am sure part of me blamed them as well. I was a little bit jealous of Marianne and Christine's friendship. The girls only knew each other for eighteen months whereas I had known Christine for much of her life. Then, for the last year, she and Marianne became inseparable.*

However, even in her grief, Margaret could not dislike the Schmidt family:

> *I know Mrs Schmidt worked very hard to keep the family together after Mr Schmidt died — he was a lovely, gentle man. Marianne was a very intelligent, beautiful girl, as was her younger sister, Trixie. When I was visiting Nan Taig, Trixie came into the house to say hello. 'You're pretty', she said to me. 'My sister, Marianne, was pretty.' She was coping with her loss the best she could.*

But with her best friend now gone, Margaret had no further contact with the Schmidt family.

As time passed and the daily Wanda headlines gradually disappeared, the general population moved on with their lives, but the Taig and Schmidt families were left wondering whether the murderer would ever be caught. Margaret was torn between the socially responsible need to bring the killer to justice and a personal desire for the whole thing to go away. 'If they caught him, all the details would be brought up again', she says. 'As far as I was concerned, I didn't want to see the billboards outside the news agencies ever again. And I don't think the Taigs did either. Christine was dead. We didn't have her any more.'

Margaret also found it very difficult to return to school at St Therese's, where the subject of Christine Sharrock's death was never really discussed. 'Sister Catherine, one of my teachers, kept a good eye on me', Margaret says. 'Whenever I was close to tears she'd ask me if I was all right but I could never talk about it.' However, when Margaret undertook a secretarial course at a Catholic business college the following year, she did not find the compassion, sensitivity and understanding she needed; she recalled one school assembly when mention was made that 'nice girls don't go to the beach and wear bikinis' and believed this to be a veiled reference to Christine Sharrock:

> *The nuns there didn't know that I knew the girls. Not all of the Sisters at business school were like that but there was this very staunch attitude among some of the senior nuns that 'the girls were in bathing costumes, they were at the beach, they were asking for it'. It was a real turning point for me. It made a significant mark on my life and turned me away from the Catholic Church.*

A childhood pact she made with Christine also shook Margaret's faith:

> *Christine and I agreed at a very young age that the first one to die had to come back and tell the other one what it was like out there. When she didn't come back and tell me, I realised then that there probably wasn't a heaven. There was always that little flicker of hope … if it was possible for her to come back she would have. But she didn't.*

As an adult, Margaret was diagnosed with clinical depression and was able to begin to recognise the unburdened grief she felt for Christine:

> *When I was a teenager, nobody took me by the hand and told me that they knew how I felt because no one did know. Nan Taig, in as much as she understood how I felt, included me in her grief but I was more there for her than for myself. She was the closest person I had to grieve with but I always felt that I let her down because I moved on, got married and didn't see her as much as I should have.*

It was incredibly difficult for Margaret, having been so close to Christine and having lost her, to maintain contact with the Taig family. 'I found the whole thing so traumatic and terrible. That is probably why I didn't keep in as much contact as I should have. It was just too painful', she says.

Christine's grandmother had told Margaret the known circumstances of the girls' deaths, which compounded Margaret's pain:

> *We all had nightmares over the extent of the girls' injuries … To this day, I still have a picture in my mind [of] what happened to them on the beach. Nan was devastated that the girls were sexually assaulted. She wouldn't have it that they'd been raped before they were murdered.*

Nan Taig was also horrified that alcohol was found in Christine's body during the post mortem examination: 'It upset her so much and she couldn't come to terms with that either. We had never touched alcohol. The way it was reported in the papers, Christine was portrayed as someone I didn't know.'

As Margaret grew older she tried to maintain contact with the Taig family, but:

not as much as I could have after I got married. Christine's grandfather died three or four years after the murders and I truly believe he died of a broken heart. He was grief-stricken. Part of my own cleansing was going to Mr Taig's funeral. I wasn't able to go to Christine's but I wanted to be there.

On the day of her wedding Margaret had two bouquets made:

The wedding finished at four o'clock and the bouquet I gave away at the end of the reception in the traditional manner was the spare bouquet I had made. I later placed the bouquet that I carried with me during my wedding ceremony on Christine's gravesite before I left on my honeymoon.

Margaret's husband knew why she needed to do this; he had been her boyfriend as a teenager, had lived down the street from her in Belfield and had met Christine Sharrock. 'We went out of our way that afternoon because it was just something that I had to do on my wedding day. Christine would have been my maid of honour.'

Christine's headstone had a photograph of her embedded in it, which Margaret found 'eerie'. As time passed, the photo faded but not Margaret's memory of her friend.

Margaret stayed in touch with Christine's grandmother because she was her one source of comfort and a way to remain connected in some way with her school friend. Mrs Taig remained in her Brush Road home until she died. 'I promised to take my third child over to visit Nan but she died three weeks after I gave birth, in 1980. I have never forgiven myself for not getting over there in time to see her.'

Christine's uncle, Leslie Taig, rang Margaret about Mrs

Taig's funeral details because he knew Mrs Taig had always thought of Margaret as part of their extended family. Mrs Taig carried her grief with her for fifteen years after Christine's murder; she was buried not far from Christine's grave in Liverpool.

Christine's mother also tried to stay in touch with Margaret but this proved to be too painful for the her:

> *The last time I saw Beryl Maher was at Nan Taig's funeral and I promised her that I would go and visit her but I couldn't bring myself to do it. I am sure her daughter's death destroyed her. I tried to make contact with her five or six years ago because I always told myself that I had unfinished business with her and I should talk to her. Beryl had moved to the Central Coast but I couldn't find her in the phone book.*

One day in the early 1980s two detectives knocked on Margaret's door. They were still investigating the Wanda case and wanted any information Margaret may have had about the son of a man who worked in a fruit shop at Lakemba — someone Margaret and Christine may have spoken to on their way home from school in the early 1960s. Shocked by the jolt from the past, she let the two detectives into her home.

The possibility that the son of someone they had only minimal contact with at Lakemba would know what Christine was doing in West Ryde, follow her to a beach by train and kill her seemed ludicrous to Margaret. 'I don't believe they knew their killer', she states. 'That's what I have believed all my life.' But she did find it heartening to know the police still cared enough to be investigating the crime — that her friend was not merely a name in an old police report.

Margaret remembers that one of the detectives remarked that she obviously had a 'storybook life'. 'When I asked him what he meant, he said that I lived in a dream house on the waterfront, I was married to my childhood sweetheart and had three beautiful sons.' But there was a lot of pressure on Margaret and her husband to keep that 'storybook life' together and the marriage later ended.

Following the end of her marriage, Margaret moved to Cronulla because her sons were surfers and wanted to be near the beach. She believes that this in itself took a lot of courage. 'I never went near the sandhills at Wanda Beach but I used to spend hours staring at them', she says. She watched as a series of huge storms in the late 1980s slowly reclaimed the area where the bodies were found. Today there are no sandhills left.

'I was a bit of a mess for a while but my life has turned around now', Margaret says. Going to university, travelling overseas and forming a new relationship with a loving partner have allowed Margaret to move forward in her life. By her own admission, she would not have been able to deal with her own 'sea change' all those years ago — 'I doubt I could have talked about Christine's death ten years ago', she said.

†

In January 1986, in the week leading up to the twenty-first anniversary of the deaths of Christine Sharrock and Marianne Schmidt, the Wanda Beach murder case was again front page news at the *Daily Mirror*. In an article largely based on a 1969 documentary by former Channel 10 journalist Steve Raymond (see Chapter 12), Marianne's mother, Elizabeth, was quoted as saying:

Marianne was always something special to us all … She was the second child in the family and the kids depended on her a lot, as I was ill at the time and their father had died six months earlier … After her murder, it was a whole different life. There were always police and reporters around and people watching and staring. For me there was no real life. There was just the realisation that I had to bring up six children, do the right thing so that one day they could stand on their own feet. I just tried to do my best.[3]

In a May 2003 interview for this book, journalist Steve Raymond recalled:

Mrs Schmidt was in hospital when it happened and I don't think she ever recovered. She felt like she wasn't in control. It impacted on the kids in that they didn't have an adult figure to guide them through that period and therefore you have to be a little forgiving about whether Helmut looked as if he was reacting as he should because it was his *sister.*

Mrs Schmidt told me that no sooner had she succeeded in moving the focus from Marianne to her other children, that she'd turn a corner and be confronted with blazing headlines about the murders and the two girls' faces staring out from the front page. No one is ever charged over your child's murder and no final chapter written … one can only imagine what it would do to you.

Mrs Schmidt admitted that her nerves 'completely went on [her] after the murder'. She was in a strange country and could not speak the language well; she had no husband or adult family in Australia: 'There was just nobody to help … When I took the children out, people would point and stare.

We felt like freaks.'

The children had lost a sister, she conceded, but nobody knew how she felt having lost a child in those circumstances:

No one deserves to die like that. When I saw the police photographs of Marianne I couldn't believe what [the killer] had done — it was shocking. I could never accept how it happened … why she had to die like that. It was the worst thing that could happen to anyone.

Worst of all, Elizabeth Schmidt had to tell her children that their sister was never coming home: 'They didn't know or even suspect she was dead, just that she hadn't come home yet.' Mrs Schmidt was driven home from hospital on Wednesday, 13 January 1965 — the day after the bodies of Marianne and Christine were found buried in the sandhills at Wanda — to tell her younger children the grim news: 'Most of them were just too little to realise what had really happened. It took them years to realise the circumstances.' For the sake of the children, Mrs Schmidt had to be strong: 'I couldn't let them see what it was doing to me. I couldn't afford to go to pieces. I had to be strong for their sake. The children couldn't talk about it. They blocked it our completely'.

Before Marianne's death, the family home in Brush Road had been 'very happy', the children 'singing and dancing'; 'It was never like that afterwards.' It was as if the childhood of each of Marianne's siblings ended the day she was murdered: 'We all stopped trusting people. All we had was each other. It was as if we were isolated on our own little island.' Most hurtful was speculation that the Schmidts had been paid money by Sydney newspapers for exclusive stories: 'We have never received anything but heartbreak out of what happened … all we have ever wanted is to be left alone'.

In January 1986 Mrs Schmidt also made the following appeal:

> *It's time for the [public] fascination to stop. It's time for people to let go of what happened. Every year the story is revived. It will never end for us, but we must be allowed to let it be forgotten by others.*

But one nagging thought ate away at her peace of mind — she could never understand why the girls were murdered:

> *It is not so important to know who did it, but why … What really keeps me going is the need to see how it ends. I just hope I am alive long enough to see the killer brought to justice and for him to tell me why he did such a thing. I think he has to one day face what he did and be punished. If he has a conscience and is able to distinguish between fantasy and reality, he must one day confess, even if it is on his deathbed.*

The only known interview provided by one of the Schmidt children in the years after their sister's death came from Norbert, the youngest of the group who went to Cronulla on 11 January 1965 and the one sibling police did not interview in their investigation because of his age. In January 1986, when he spoke to Tony Barnao, Norbert Schmidt was twenty-seven years old with a family of his own:

> *I remember Marianne and Christine walking away from us to walk back to Cronulla Beach to pick up some of our belongings that we had left there. I can still hear them laughing when we called out that they were heading in the wrong direction.*[4]

Norbert admitted that when he forced himself to go back to Wanda Beach about ten years after his sister's death, 'everything seemed a lifetime away' from the day his oldest sister took them to that beach:

It took me years to come to terms with it … I always feel a terrible sense of loss whenever I think about it — we all do. I always resented the fact that it had happened to us. None of us talked about it, except when it was in the papers.

What bound the family together was the fact that they each knew how the other siblings felt. The Schmidt children drew ranks in order to survive their ordeal. 'We all managed to come through it', Norbert said, 'but only because mum was so strong and loving. Without her I don't know what would have happened to us.' In the years since this interview, the Schmidt family has steadfastly maintained its silence on the matter of Marianne's death.

Elizabeth Schmidt never did see her daughter's killer brought to justice. In 1979, she finally moved from the family home in Brush Road, West Ryde, and after her children left home to start their own families, she lived alone for the final years of her life. Every Sunday for fifteen years after her daughter's death, Mrs Schmidt visited Rookwood Cemetery and placed flowers in Marianne's vault in the Lutheran Church chapel. Towards the end of her life, she used to visit Rookwood 'about four times a year when [she felt] the need to be with her'. She also visited Christine's grave at Liverpool cemetery but gradually stopped that practice when it became too much for her.

When she passed away, the Wanda Beach investigation remained unresolved.

†

At a school reunion at St Therese's Catholic Girls' School in Lakemba in the early 1990s, special mention was made of the fact that Christine Sharrock was not there to celebrate with the rest of the former students. Margaret Kavazos recalls the reunion:

> *Everyone met up with their friends, but of course my best friend wasn't there … our former principal who is now in her eighties, made special mention in her speech that we had all gone through a personal trauma all those years ago. There was a group of twelve of us who had started kindergarten together and had gone through to Year 9 and only one of us wasn't there that night — Christine.*

'I still think about Christine. I have a little picture of her that her grandmother sent to me.' Margaret holds a faded image of a petite girl, dressed in the fashion of her time, attending her first wedding — that of her Uncle Les. 'Each year I remember her birthday and I remind myself that this beautiful life really existed.'

CHAPTER 9

FALSE CONFESSIONS

'A number of young men admitted to the Wanda Beach murders. When persons are mentally deficient or unstable, they read and see articles in the press and on the news, and they apply what is reported to themselves. It would have been easy for us to just go off and charge any of them with the murders, believing that they were telling us the truth. But once we investigated what they told us, we came to the conclusion that they weren't responsible because what they said didn't marry with the crime scene.'

Former Detective Sergeant Keith Paull, who worked on the Wanda Beach murder investigation from 1965 to 1973

In February 1965 — six weeks after the bodies of Christine Sharrock and Marianne Schmidt were found buried in the sandhills at Wanda Beach — Sydney detectives were contacted by Tasmanian police regarding a potential suspect in the case. Norma Parker (not her real name), a 44-year-old woman living in suburban Hobart, had informed local police of the recent arrival of her nephew from Sydney, and of her grave fears about the mental state of the 22-year-old.

On 23 February, Mrs Parker had answered a knock on her door to find a young man — dishevelled but vaguely familiar — standing in front of her.

'Don't you know who I am?' the young man asked. 'No, I don't know who you are', Mrs Parker replied.

'I am Levon [not his real name] and you are my aunty.'

Despite the fact that she did not immediately recognise him, Mrs Parker invited the youth inside.

'I've just come down from Sydney', Levon told his aunt, adding, 'they have been knocking me around up there'. After visiting some other relatives, he had stayed at a hotel for a week before visiting his aunt. He did not have any clothing or money with him at the time but said he was waiting for a £30 pay cheque to arrive from Sydney. Although by her own recollection she had not seen the young man since he was thirteen, Mrs Parker gave him something to eat and invited him to stay the night.

The next morning, as Mrs Parker made Levon breakfast, he looked through the newspaper; she asked if he was going to look for a job but he did not answer. Levon later commented that there was 'nothing in the paper about me today', appearing upset as he continued to read and reread the newspaper. Later that afternoon, he asked his aunt if she had ever been to Cronulla.

'Yes', she said, 'and so have those boys of mine. We used to go for a swim there when they were small.'

'A funny thing', Levon said. 'I was on the beach the day the murders happened. I was only a mile away from where it happened. It's a wonder the cops haven't questioned me about it.'

'What murders are you talking about?' his aunt asked.

'The Wanda Beach murders, where the two girls got murdered', he said. 'It wasn't always called Wanda Beach was it? We knew it as Cronulla.' 'Wanda Beach is a little beach that runs off Cronulla Beach', he explained. Later that day Levon again brought up the subject, telling his aunt, 'It's a wonder they didn't blame me and question me for doing it because I left the state.'

The next day, Levon's unusual behaviour continued: he pored over the newspaper and again commented that there was nothing in it about him; he declined to run an errand for his aunt to the local shops because there were 'too many cops down there' and they might recognise him. The following day when he was again discussing the murders he appeared worried; one of the Wanda Beach headlines, 'BOY HELD', had found its way to Tasmania, and Levon told his aunt: 'they only think they've got him but they haven't. They've got the wrong man.'

Each day Levon looked through the newspapers, becoming increasingly agitated. He also began playing with a large bread knife, telling his aunt he liked knives that were 'big and sharp'. More worryingly, he also began to play inappropriately with Mrs Parker's ten-year-old daughter, wrestling with her and pinning her to the ground. When Mrs Parker arranged for her nephew to pick fruit on a nearby farm to earn some money, she also contacted the local police about her concerns.

On 9 March, Detective Sergeants Keith Paull and Fred Shaw — who had both been working on the Wanda Beach murder case from the day the bodies were discovered — travelled to Hobart to interview Levon. They were briefed on arrival by a local detective who had interviewed the young man three days earlier. Levon had told this detective he was at Wanda Beach on 11 January with a woman named Margaret and that he had met a man there named Angelo, who had murdered the two girls.

When Paull and Shaw put this scenario to him, Levon recanted it, telling them he had not been at Wanda Beach and that Angelo was the name of a work colleague in Sydney he did not particularly like because he was a 'new Australian'.

The detectives then asked Levon if he had ever had a conversation with any person 'in which that person has admitted to killing Marianne Schmidt and Christine Sharrock on Wanda Beach'. Levon said he had not.

'Our inquiries … revealed that you were not at work on

January 11 1965', the detectives began. 'We have been told that a telephone message was received at their office that day stating that you were sick and not reporting to work. Can you assist us as to your whereabouts on January 11?'

'I was home in bed', Levon said. 'I had a sore throat. I got my brother to ring up at about 10 to 10.'

'Our inquiries revealed that you did not report for work the following day either.'

'I was home that day too, still with a sore throat.'

'Do you recall if you have visited Wanda Beach at any time?'

'I don't think so.'

'Have you ever visited Cronulla Beach?'

'I don't think that I have.'

Paull and Shaw ended the interview, arranging to see Levon again the following day. They asked him if he knew his blood grouping and if the shoes he was wearing at the time — a pair of black pointed shoes — were the pair he wore on 11 January. Levon told the detectives he did not know his blood grouping and signed a consent form for police to obtain a sample; he also confirmed the shoes were the pair he wore on the day of the murders.

By the following day, Levon's story had changed once more: 'I *was* down at Wanda Beach on the day the two girls were killed but I didn't see Angelo down there … What I told you about Angelo last night [about his not being there] is true.'

When asked how he travelled to Wanda Beach on 11 January, Levon replied that he 'went to Redfern railway station and bought a ticket and got off at Cronulla'. This was the same route Christine and the Schmidts had taken. Had he followed them there, or had he merely read it in a newspaper?

'What time did you arrive at Cronulla?'

'A bit after twelve', he said. This would place him at Wanda in plenty of time to commit the murders.

'Can you tell us what your activities were on that day after arriving at Cronulla?'

'I got off the train and I had a look at some clothing shops near the railway … I walked down to the rocks at Cronulla and after that I walked along the beach to Wanda.'

'How were you dressed that day?'

'Blue cardigan, chequered shirt and grey trousers, and the black shoes that you took from me last night.' A man's shoeprint had been found in the sand near the bodies.

'Can you assist us as to what you did at the Wanda section of the beach that day?'

'I saw the two girls there and I asked one for a root and she said no. So I pulled my knife out and I stabbed one and the other one tried to get away and I threw my knife at her and hit her in the back.' Could this have been how the two girls died? It was a romanticised account of possible events.

The detectives then explained to Levon that before they asked him any further questions they needed him to be aware of his rights and that anything he said could be used as evidence against him.

'Yes, but there are some things I can't remember', Levon replied. He then answered 'I don't remember' to the next ten questions until Paull asked, 'What happened to the knife … you say … you threw at one of the girls?'

'I don't know. I think I threw it away in the sand down there.'

'What type of knife was that?'

'A Jim Bowie knife.' This was a common type of knife in circulation among teenagers at the time — made popular by a 1950s television production on the life of the American frontiersman — but did not usually have a serrated edge.

'How long had you had possession of that knife?'

'About six or eight months.'

'Can you describe that knife?

'The blade is about 4 inches long and a little bit bigger than half an inch wide.' This description did not match a Bowie knife.

'Where were you carrying the knife on your person on January 11?' 'It was in a pouch down the front of my pants.'

'Can you tell me if any other conversation took place between yourself and the … two girls on Wanda beach on January 11?'

Levon then broke down and cried, babbling that what he had told the detectives was all lies. 'I wasn't down at the beach at all that day', he said. 'I was home in bed with a sore throat and I got my brother to ring up work and say I wouldn't be in. He can tell you where I was that day. I was home the next day too.'

The detectives told Levon they would confirm his statement about being at home on 11 January by interviewing his brother in Sydney.

Levon was crying forcefully now, his head buried in his hands: 'What I told you about killing the girls was lies … What I told you I did down there was what I read in the papers. I get mixed up and I tell lies.'

The detectives made their long trip home no closer to solving the Wanda case. Police later confirmed that Levon had been at home with his brother on the day Christine and Marianne were murdered. The detectives' journey to Tasmania had been a wasted exercise and even at this early stage in the investigation, police could not afford to waste time chasing false leads.

✝

Detective Sergeant Cecil (Cec) Johnson, came into the murder investigation in the weeks following the discovery of the girls' bodies at Wanda Beach. Among police colleagues Johnson was known as a gentleman; an earnest, quietly spoken professional who took his job and the societal expectations that came with it very seriously. At about 10.30 a.m. on 19 February 1965, Johnson went to the Yasmar Children's Court in suburban Ashfield to interview Caleb (not his real name), a sixteen-year-old youth awaiting sentencing for theft. Caleb had spoken often, and intimately, about the Wanda case, and was reported to the police by his employer when he disappeared from work after just two weeks. The night before he interviewed Caleb, Johnson spoke with the boy's uncle and was able to form an understanding of Caleb's home life.

Caleb was deserted by his father at the age of three along with his four siblings. When he was ten years old his mother moved to the country to live with a man and left Caleb in the care of an aunt. In the ensuing years, Caleb's mother had a number of children with this man and did not make contact with Caleb again until she returned to live in Sydney five years later.

In Sydney, Caleb's mother saw her son on a fortnightly basis, and noticed that the boy was prone to exaggerate everyday incidents and was generally untruthful with her. While Caleb had never shown any violence towards his mother, he had threatened to use his Bowie knife to 'cut up' the man who had taken her away from him. The knife was 6 or 7 inches long and was carried in a sheath and belt around his waist.

In September 1964 at the age of sixteen, Caleb was placed under the guardianship of his uncle and went to live with him in Kurnell. While the uncle thought the teenager 'a good kid' in his company, he regarded the boy as something of a liar. On many occasions Caleb recounted 'true' stories to his uncle that were later found to be false. Having already left school, Caleb was encouraged by his uncle to find a job and despite having little difficulty in obtaining work, only lasted a week or two. Caleb's unsettled state, the uncle told Johnson the night before the boy was questioned, usually followed bad news about his mother, brother or sisters.

Johnson began his interview with Caleb by asking the boy if he remembered what he did on Monday, 11 January and whether he had discussed the subject with his uncle.

'Yes, my uncle remembered that I got home about two minutes to twelve that day. I went out in the morning to get a job and I got home just before the twelve o'clock siren blew at the Kurnell oil refinery.'

'How do you particularly remember what you did on that day?' Johnson asked.

'It's about the murders at Wanda, isn't it?' Caleb replied. Johnson nodded. 'Well, when we read about it in the papers the next day I just remembered that I was home', the boy continued. 'What did you do that day?' Johnson prodded.

Caleb told Johnson he went to the local employment office in the morning and then on to a job interview at a transport company in Kirrawee. Caleb obtained the job as a removalist's offsider and then returned to his uncle's house. 'As far as I can remember I stayed home all day. I didn't leave home until the next day when I went to work.'

'Did you go down to the beach that day?' Johnson asked.

The boy hesitated for a moment before answering: 'Come to think of it, I didn't get a lift home. I caught the train to Cronulla and I walked around the beach.'

'Would you like to tell me exactly what you did that day?' Johnson said.

'I caught the 11.30 train from Kirrawee to Cronulla and I walked down through the park and on to the beach and I walked right along the beach towards Kurnell.'

'Did you walk past Wanda Beach?'

'Yes. I walked for about a mile past Wanda and I sat on a sandhill for a while. I don't remember what happened after that. The next thing I remember I was walking back towards Wanda and I walked down on to Kurnell Road and I got a lift from a passing motorist.'

'What time did you get home?'

'It must have been just after half past one because *Coronation Street* was on TV and it starts at half past one.'

'Can you remember how long you remained at the sandhill before starting to walk back to Wanda?'

'Well, I would have got there sometime between twelve and half past, so I must have been up there for about half an hour.' At this, the boy covered his face with his hands and began to cry.

When Johnson asked why he was crying, Caleb replied: 'I think I might have done something terrible. I think I might have killed those girls but I don't remember.' The boy's story did not ring true, but the unexplained gaps were worrying. Was the boy schizophrenic? Could he be capable of violence? Johnson contacted Detective Inspector Ned Haines, the officer in charge of the Wanda investigation, and asked him to join the interview. Caleb asked for a piece of paper so he could draw 'what happened' at Wanda Beach on 11 January. At this stage Johnson informed Caleb of his rights and reminded him that anything he said could be given in evidence against him. Caleb said he understood this and added, 'I will draw you what happened and show you what I did … if I did it.' The boy began to sketch a plan, making certain marks and labelling what the marks meant. 'If I did it, this is what I would have done', he said, pointing to the plan.

When Haines arrived in the company of Detective Sergeants Bob Walton and Alan Yates, Johnson took them aside and apprised them of his conversation with Caleb. Haines then addressed the boy: 'Detective Sergeant Johnson has informed us that you told him you were on the beach at Wanda on January 11 … and that you indicated to him that you may have been responsible for the death of the two girls.'

'Yes, I told him that.'

'Did you kill the two girls?' Haines asked.

'I can't remember, but I was sitting on the beach and I seemed to go to sleep and when I woke up I thought I had done something terrible or had a terrible dream.'

'What terrible thing do you think you might have done?'

'I think I may have killed the girls.'

'What makes you think that?'

'When I saw their pictures in the paper they looked familiar, and I thought I might have seen them somewhere before. I mentioned it to my uncle.'

Johnson took shorthand notes as Caleb recounted the story he told Johnson, and at the conclusion of the interview Johnson read his shorthand notes back to Caleb, who confirmed the notes and signed his name on each page. The boy also drew a sketch of a knife he claimed was the murder weapon.

Caleb later appeared before the Yasmar Children's Court on various theft charges unrelated to the murders and was remanded until 26 February. In a vestibule outside the courtroom Caleb spoke to his uncle about the conversation he had with the Wanda detectives, during which the boy's uncle cried out: 'You didn't do it. You didn't do it. Tell me you didn't do it, did you?'

Caleb collapsed in a chair beside his uncle and said, 'I did it.'

'You did?'

'Yes, I did do it and I'm sorry and I am grateful for everything that you have done for me.' They then held each other and cried together.

Shortly after this encounter, detectives took Caleb in

a police car to Cronulla police station. On the way there they asked the boy if he had returned to the scene after the murders. Caleb replied that he had and, when asked if he knew the area well, replied: 'I ought to … There is something that makes you want to go back. It's a compulsion. I don't know what it is. I often think that I would like to run my mother through.'

Walton asked Caleb why he was so hostile towards his mother, to which Caleb replied bitterly:

> *You don't know what it's like to have been abandoned by your mother … For a long time I didn't know where my mother was. Then I found out where she was and when she came and saw me, she promised to send me a present for my birthday. I went to the letterbox every day and waited for a parcel to arrive and when it didn't come by Christmas I knew that she didn't intend to send it and I was back where I started.*

The boy began to cry and buried his head in his hands; his life was unravelling before the detectives' eyes. During the drive Caleb appeared to fall asleep momentarily and shortly after complained of feeling ill.

When at Cronulla police station, Caleb agreed to prepare a written statement, telling the detectives, 'I will be glad to get it off my mind'. He also answered a list of written questions the detectives gave him, before asking if he had to sign them.

'Yes, if you wish to', Walton replied. 'That is, if you think that it is true.'

'You don't think I would write a thing like that if it wasn't true, do you?' Caleb said. He signed both documents and agreed to draw another plan of Wanda Beach, setting out exactly how and where he had killed and buried Christine and Marianne. The sketched plan of the murder scene, however, did not agree with the known facts of the crime, so in order to ascertain the validity of Caleb's claims, the detectives took him to Wanda Beach shortly after 4.30 p.m. the same day.

Inaccuracies began to show in Caleb's story. The first came after Caleb showed the detectives where he allegedly first met Christine and Marianne on the day they died; Caleb described Monday, 11 January as a 'lovely, sunny day, with a gentle breeze blowing' — it was well known that 11 January was a windy day and the seas so rough that Cronulla Beach was closed.

Walton then asked Caleb to take them to the place he had killed the girls; he led them to the wrong place, three or four hundred yards north of the murder scene. 'This is where it started and this is where it finished', Caleb said authoritatively. 'I started having intercourse with the little one and the other one was standing alongside momentarily.

Then she started to run and I chased her. I chased her over there.' He indicated a southerly direction, back towards Wanda rather than the northerly direction where Christine Sharrock tried to flee her killer.

'I caught her and I grabbed her around the head with my right hand and I cut her throat with my left hand. Then I grabbed her under the arms and I dragged her back over here and I buried the two of them there.' Caleb indicated a depression in the sand about ten feet long and two feet deep. 'I always dig a deep grave', he added.

'How deep did you dig the grave?' Walton asked.

'About six feet deep', he said. The detectives knew the girls were buried in a shallow grave. Caleb's claim that he placed the girls' bodies side by side in the grave was also incorrect. As further details were given, Caleb's lack of involvement in the crime became very clear. He stated that he did not hit either girl on the back of the head, nor did he sexually interfere with Marianne Schmidt — the killer had perpetrated both these acts. His description of the girls' clothing was also incorrect and he stated that he had never seen a girl wearing a sanitary napkin — Christine Sharrock was wearing one at the time of her death.

Although Caleb's depiction of the crime was littered with inaccuracies, the detectives allowed him to continue and asked him about his movements immediately following the murders.

'What did you do with the knife afterwards?' 'I threw it in the water over there', he said. 'Did you get any blood on your clothing?'

'I took my trousers off before I started to have intercourse but I got blood on my shirt. I took my shoes and socks off before I went into the water. I washed the blood off and I walked back to Wanda and then to the school turn-off and I got a lift there in a black Holden.'

'What time do you estimate you arrived back at the vicinity of the Wanda clubhouse?'

'Ten past one', the boy said, adding that he remembered looking at the clubhouse clock. The detectives then walked Caleb back towards the Wanda Surf Club. They stopped at the murder scene and asked the boy if the area had any special significance for him. 'No', he said, 'I have never been here before.'

When they returned to Cronulla police station Walton informed Caleb that some of the details he had given did not agree with the facts of the case. 'Well, that's the way I would have done it if I had done it', Caleb told them. 'All I remember is that I was on the beach like I said, and I did see two girls on the beach and sat down.'

'Did you have any physical contact with the girls Sharrock and Schmidt that day?' Walton asked.

'I don't think I did', the boy replied. 'If I did, I don't remember.'

'Can you tell us what happened to the sheath of the knife … you say … you threw away that day?' He did not throw it in the water, the boy told them; it was at home, in his room, or was it in the shed? He could not remember.

When the detectives questioned Caleb the following day, he admitted he had not gone to either Cronulla or Wanda Beach the day the girls were murdered. When pressed as to why he lied in his initial interview, Caleb said: 'I got all mixed up. I was upset. But what I told them is what I think I would have done if I killed the girls.' Caleb then wrote a statement to this effect.

When his mother visited him the following Monday, Caleb asked if his name had appeared in the newspapers: 'Can we go to a newsagent and see what kind of headlines I made?'.

✝

Five men claimed to have committed the Wanda Beach murders but their lack of knowledge of the crime scene meant that detectives could not accept their admissions. When interviewed for this book in September 2002, Keith Paull described the situation he and his fellow investigators found themselves in:

> *When persons are mentally deficient or unstable, they read and see articles in the press and on the news, and they apply what is reported to themselves. It would have been easy for us to just go off and charge any of them with the murders, believing that they were telling us the truth. But once we investigated what they told us, we came to the conclusion that they weren't responsible because what they said didn't marry with the crime scene …*
>
> *I spent more time on the investigation than any of the others and prepared the case for the coroner … I found the*

original investigation to be very sincere. We were committed to not stuffing up the inquiry for the sake of obtaining a quick arrest. We wouldn't have done the case any favours to present the wrong person before the courts and share the more private details of the case with the public, thereby tainting any subsequent investigation.

Above: The Schmidt family arrives at the Metropolitan Funeral Home, Burwood, for Marianne's funeral on 20 January 1965. (From left) Peter, Wolfgang, Hans, Norbert, Helmut, Elizabeth and Trixie.

Below: Helmut and Trixie Schmidt flank their mother, Elizabeth, at the funeral of their sister, Marianne.

Above: The funeral of Marianne Schmidt at the Metropolitan Funeral Home, Burwood, 20 January 1965.

Below: The funeral of Christine Sharrock at St Michael's Catholic Church, Meadowbank, 20 January 1965.

Above: Christine Sharrock's mother, Beryl Maher, and her husband, Barry, leave Christine's funeral, 20 January 1965.

Left: Christine's grandmother, Jeanette Taig, with whom Christine lived in Brush Road, West Ryde, January 1965.

Above: A detective takes Wolfgang, Trixie and Peter Schmidt back to Cronulla on 13 January 1965, retracing the children's fateful journey to Wanda.

Below: Sydney detectives walk Wolfgang, Trixie and Peter Schmidt past Cronulla Beach while retracing the Schmidt's 11 January journey to Wanda Beach.

Above: Piccadilly Arcade, Wollongong — the scene of the brutal murder of 57-year-old Wilhelmina Kruger on 26 January 1966. A link between the Kruger murder and the Wanda crime was suspected but has not been proved.

Below: Police examine the body of nineteen-year-old Carolyn Orphin, discovered on the side of the Mount Ousley By-Pass Road, Wollongong, on 11 June 1966. Alan Bassett later confessed to murdering Orphin.

The painting (above) Alan Bassett painted and gave to former Wanda detective Cec Johnson in 1975, and (below) an artist's impression of the 'clues' hidden in Bassett's painting. The 'clues' allegedly point to four murders – Sharrock, Schmidt, Kruger and Dowlingkoa – and the possible murderer's face (etched into the tree stump).

Cat and Mouse. Former Wanda
detective Cec Johnson (above)
was haunted by the identity of the
Wanda Beach murderer. Johnson
died in 1980, believing the murderer
to be Alan Bassett (right) and
pursued a confession from Bassett
for decades after the crime. Bassett
is pictured in a 1977 *Daily Mirror*
story at Morisset Psychiatric
Hospital, where he was sent as a
21-year-old after being convicted
of murdering nineteen-year-old
Carolyn Orphin.

Daily Mirror

Twenty years after the murder of Christine Sharrock and Marianne Schmidt, the Wanda Beach crime continued to make front page headlines. The murder remains unsolved and the original $20 000 reward for information leading to a conviction remains in place. This newspaper article was published on 9 January 1986.

CHAPTER 10
POSSIBLE CONNECTIONS: KRUGER AND DOWLINGKOA[1]

'There is a possibility the (Kruger) killer and the Wanda Beach killer could be the same person. This crime was committed no great distance from the locality where the two young girls were viciously attacked in January last year at Wanda Beach. On the information available to us we cannot discount the possibility Mrs Wilhelmina Kruger … met her death at the hands of the same person who is being sought for the murders at Wanda Beach.'

Detective Sergeant Dick Lendrum, speaking at a press conference in January 1966

The murders of Wilhelmina Kruger and Annya Dowlingkoa in the early months of 1966 remain two of the most horrific unsolved crimes in New South Wales. They play a part in this book because detectives working on these investigations had reason to suspect that each murder was linked not only to the other, but also to the deaths of Christine Sharrock and Marianne Schmidt at Wanda Beach twelve months earlier. This connection has never been proven, but the deaths of Kruger and Dowlingkoa, while not as well known today as the Wanda Beach murders, remain inexorably linked in time, place and motivation to the deaths of the two teenage girls at Wanda.

At 5.40 a.m. on Saturday, 29 January 1966 — the first day of the Australia Day long weekend — Wollongong butcher Thomas Fitzgibbon arrived at the Piccadilly Arcade in Crown Street to start work at 6.00 a.m. Fitzgibbon found the arcade full of steam and the lights of the shopping centre, which were usually left on during the night, switched off.[2]

At the top of an escalator at the Gladstone Avenue end of the arcade, Fitzgibbon saw an electric immersion heater boiling away in a metal cleaning bucket with the half-squeezed mop between the rollers. The cleaning lady, he thought, was using an electric element to heat the water and had perhaps wandered off somewhere and forgotten about it; but this was unlike the cleaner, whom he knew to be Wilhelmina Kruger, a woman who methodically worked to routine in the early hours of each morning. Fitzgibbon also saw a set of keys on the steps of the escalator and proceeded to follow a trail of seemingly unrelated objects — a set of false teeth that had been smashed into pieces, a man's wristwatch, a pair of women's shoes and a flowery work apron — to a set of stairs leading to the sub-basement car park. There, he tried to open a door to Gladstone Street to retrieve some equipment from his car but the door was jammed. Walking down the stairs to the car park, he found the partly naked body of 57-year-old Wilhelmina Kruger, lying in a pool of blood.

Running back to the top floor of the arcade to find a phone, Fitzgibbon shouted to a young couple standing in the street, 'Don't go down there, there's a woman down below who's been beaten up'. The three then flagged down a taxi that was dropping a fare off at the Piccadilly Arcade and the driver radioed his base and reported what he had been told about the incident. Fitzgibbon returned to the basement and felt the body for a pulse. When an ambulance arrived at 5.50 a.m., the ambulance driver noted that rigor mortis was beginning to set in.[3]

Shortly after 6.00 a.m. Detective Graham Carter of the Wollongong CIB was woken to be told of the gruesome find. Arriving at the Piccadilly Arcade forty minutes later, Carter was shown to the base of the steps leading down to the car park. The body of the woman lay on the car park floor, adjacent to the steps and only partly covered by a dress, petticoat and brassiere, which were torn and bloodstained. Carter noted a number of round holes consistent with cigarette burns in the dress and saw a smudge of blood containing the bar pattern of a man's average-size shoeprint near the victim's left foot. He found a similar shoeprint on the set of stairs leading down to the basement, and a herringbone shoeprint near the top of the stairs leading up from the basement.

Carter then examined the wooden fuse box in the sub-basement: it was open and appeared to have been tampered with. Henry Mandel, the superintendent of the Piccadilly Arcade, later confirmed that a wire in the fuse box had either been tampered with or removed — this was the only explanation for the lights going off that morning. The fuse box was dusted for fingerprints, but none were found.

Constable Barry Wharton, who was stationed at Wollongong at the time, arrived at the Piccadilly Arcade at about 6.00 a.m. According to the constable's evidence at the coronial inquest, he found a clump of 'colourless' hair — either grey or bleached blond — on the escalator leading up from the basement. The ends of the hairs had small white sacs attached to them, suggesting they had been ripped straight from a head. Checking the body lying on the concrete floor, he could see that the victim's hair was dyed reddish-brown. When he returned to take a sample of the hair from the escalator some time later, the strands had blown away. A search of the area was made, but the evidence was lost.

At the time of her death, Wilhelmina Kruger was separated from her husband and lived with one of her adult sons and her de facto husband, 38-year-old Stan Dawson, in the Wollongong suburb of Gwynneville.[4] She had separated and reunited with her husband, Albert — a carpenter who lived in Broken Hill — on many occasions during their marriage and was known to have had relationships with a number of different men. Police theorised[5] that if her death was a crime of passion, there were certainly several suspects. One of her sons later told police that his mother drank in moderation but did not smoke: the cigarette holes in her dress could not be explained.

On the day Kruger died her de facto husband drove her to work, dropping her off at the Gladstone Avenue entrance to Piccadilly Arcade shortly after 2.00 a.m. Dawson turned the lights on for Kruger at the shopping centre fuse box, which was in working order. Milkman Alan Hovey later told detectives that he often saw Kruger arrive for work at the Gladstone Avenue entrance to the Piccadilly Arcade. At 4.30 on the morning of 29 January, Hovey was delivering milk in nearby Rawlinson Avenue when he saw the lights of the Piccadilly Arcade flicker off. At the same time, he heard a screech of tyres coming from the direction of the arcade. Local policeman Constable John Dooley reported that he was in a police patrol car in Gladstone Avenue at 3.20 a.m. when he saw a woman outside the florist shop of the Piccadilly Arcade carrying something, possibly a bucket — this was most likely Kruger going about her duties. He also noticed the lights in the basement and Crown Street floors of the arcade were off. Dooley drove up the ramp to the motel on top of the Piccadilly Arcade and completed a routine search of the cars in the motel car park. On his way down the ramp, he saw the woman near the ramp leading down to the basement area of the building. The time was then 3.40 a.m. The last official sighting of Kruger before she was murdered was by nightwatchman William Simpson, who spoke to Kruger at about 4.00 a.m. at the entrance to the arcade.

Wilhelmina Kruger's employer described her as an obstinate woman who worked to routine. When she began work, usually between 1.00 a.m. and 2.00 a.m., the first thing she did was switch on the lights in the fuse box. She took two-and-a-half hours to clean the Crown Street level, finishing near the escalator that led down to the Gladstone Street level.

Police conjectured that the murder was premeditated and that the killer possibly knew the layout of the Piccadilly Arcade, as well as Kruger's working routine and where to take her to commit the murder uninterrupted.[6] Kruger always finished work by 6.00 a.m., when she stopped for a meal — the killer attacked her between 4.00 a.m. and 5.00 a.m., in the middle of her shift. No effort had been made to hide the body; it was left at the base of the stairs where it would be found by people arriving at the arcade for work.

Although it was obvious to detectives that Kruger had been battered to death with a blunt instrument and mutilated with a knife or other sharp implement, no weapon was found at the crime scene. Doctor Godfrey Oettle, the Government Medical Officer from Sydney, also found that 'some form of strangulation had been carried out'. Specimens were taken from the body to determine whether, as police assumed, the woman had been sexually assaulted.

The post-mortem examination conducted by Doctor EM Diment, the Wollongong Government Medical Officer, found that Wilhelmina Kruger had suffered two black eyes, knife wounds to the neck and head, a burst heart muscle and multiple other injuries. Police were able to determine that Kruger was knocked unconscious while she mopped the top floor of the arcade, dragged from behind down the escalator and stairs and then manually strangled and mutilated with a knife. Rope burns on the front of her neck were consistent with her being dragged from behind with a ropelike object, possibly her own stockings, wrapped around her neck. In his official report, Diment also stated that Kruger's heart had been ruptured by a 'tremendous blow to the centre of her chest, probably by a knee'; this in itself was an unusual injury in a murder case and the same injury would be repeated in another murder twelve months later (see Chapter 11).

The autopsy could not determine whether Kruger had been raped, and police kept the details of the sexual attack on Kruger within official circles. However, it was later reported that her nipples had been bitten off and she had been disembowelled.[7]

From the outset, detectives working on the case, many of whom were brought in from Sydney and had worked on the Wanda Beach murders the previous year, knew they needed a major break to solve the case.[8] They had no suspect, no motive and no eyewitnesses to the attack, and the case threatened to be sucked into the same black hole that had consumed the Wanda investigation. 'We feel that without the assistance of the public, this crime could go unsolved', Detective Sergeant Dick Lendrum, from Sydney CIB, told the *Illawarra Mercury* in the early days of the investigation. 'We want to interview anyone in the locality where Mrs Kruger was attacked between midnight on Friday and 6.00 a.m. on Saturday.' Superintendent David Watts of the Wollongong Police made his case for public assistance as plain as he could: 'Everyone should realise that there is a sex maniac at large and the same thing could happen again, although I dread the thought.'

Some people did come forward with information. Roy Keast, a Victorian truck driver, told police he was booked into the Piccadilly Motel, directly above the shopping arcade, on the morning of the murder. He, his wife and four friends drove past the arcade at about 3.50 a.m. after driving all night from Traralgon. Keast was unable to find the motel so asked directions from a man sitting in a utility truck in Keira Street behind the arcade. Keast saw a cleaning woman with a mop and bucket — undoubtedly Kruger — as he first drove past the arcade but saw no other person near her; Keast and his passengers again noticed the cleaning woman at about 4.00 a.m. when driving into the entrance of the arcade. When the group was booking into the motel ten minutes later, they heard the screech of tyres that the local milkman later reported.

Thomas Crilly, another taxi driver working in Gladstone Avenue on the morning of the murder, also noted the cream-coloured utility truck with a painted canopy between 3.00 a.m. and 4.00 a.m. Basil Galick, the taxi driver who radioed for help after the discovery of the body, later told police he was parked at the taxi rank opposite the Tattersall's Hotel in Crown Street at 4.00 a.m. when he noticed a man behaving suspiciously; the man was about 6 feet tall and was walking along Crown Street towards the arcade. The man walked slowly along Crown Street, stopping at the nearby Ironworkers' Building for a moment before crossing to the other side. Police were unable to establish the identity of the 'tall man'.

Herta Trucis of Mount St Thomas (who cleaned a nearby office block) walked with her husband to work, up Gladstone Street and back down Crown Street at 4.45 a.m. on 29 January, and noticed the Piccadilly Arcade lights were switched off. Trucis knew Kruger cleaned the arcade during this time and told her husband that it was unusually dark. She also noticed that the entrance to the arcade looked uncleaned. Continuing down the street, she saw a young man running through a lane alongside the Tattersall's Hotel, about 100 yards from the Piccadilly Arcade. The young man was wearing blue jeans with a studded belt.

At 4.55 on the morning of the murder, 68-year-old pensioner Joseph Brookfield was standing at the front gate of his house in nearby Osborne Street waiting for his newspaper to arrive when he saw an old utility truck travelling toward him. According to Brookfield, the driver was between 25 and 30 years old and drove 'like a frenzied animal'. 'I was shocked at the look on his face', Brookfield told detectives. 'He had a horrible appearance.' When the utility was about 75 feet from Brookfield's house, the driver did a sudden U-turn and headed back up to Gladstone Street. 'I never saw that chap before and I never wanted to see him again', said Brookfield, who was so shocked by the expression on the man's face that he did not see what type of vehicle it was. As best as he could remember, it was an old utility, grey or cream coloured, with a canopy on the back. Detectives working on the case identified five men they wanted to speak to regarding Wilhelmina Kruger's death and released the following details through the media:

- the driver of a cream-coloured vehicle with a wooden canopy over the back that was parked in Gladstone Avenue, Wollongong, about 50 yards from the entrance to the Piccadilly Arcade at about 5.00 a.m.;
- the driver of a dark van seen in Gladstone Avenue, Wollongong, at 4.30 a.m. and that stopped opposite the Dairy Farmers' Milk Cooperative;
- a man sitting in the driver's seat of a one-ton utility

> truck with a canopy over the back that was parked outside the Crown Street Carpets store in Keira Street at about 4.00 a.m.;
>
> - a tall man walking in a northerly direction towards Keira Street about 4.00 a.m.; and
> - a youth running down a lane behind the Tattersall's Hotel at 4.45 a.m.[9]

The driver of the one-ton utility truck was ultimately found and cleared of any involvement in the crime, but the others, especially the 'tall man' and the youth running behind the Tattersall's Hotel, were never identified.

Detectives appealed to members of the public to come forward with any information about the following: persons seen washing bloodstains from vehicles or clothing; hitchhikers entering or leaving Wollongong on 29 January; persons unexpectedly absent from their home or place of work on the night of Friday, 28 January, or the morning of Saturday, 29 January; or persons who had suddenly departed since this time. As was the case in the Wanda investigation, police also checked a list of the criminally insane and psychiatric patients who may have escaped from mental institutions, but with no result.

Acting on a report that a man was seen behaving suspiciously at North Beach the day after the murder, police searched a 100-yard strip of beach for evidence that may have been connected to the crime. Could there have been a subconscious link with the Wanda Beach case — earthmoving equipment was also used to sift sand for clues on that occasion — and a feeling that if the killer was the Wanda Beach murderer, what better place to hide the bloodstained clothing than a beach? The search, however, proved fruitless.

Detective Sergeant Dick Lendrum admitted at a press conference that there was a 'possibility the local killer and the Wanda Beach killer could be the same person'.[10] He described the murder of Wilhelmina Kruger and those of Christine Sharrock and Marianne Schmidt as all 'cases of vicious attacks' and reminded the press that the Piccadilly Arcade crime was committed 'no great distance from the locality where the two young girls were viciously attacked in January last year at Wanda Beach. On the information available to us we cannot discount the possibility Mrs Wilhelmina Kruger … met her death at the hands of the same person who is being sought for the murder at Wanda Beach.'

Among the Sydney detectives called into the Kruger investigation were Detective Sergeant Keith Paull (in charge of the Wanda case at that time) and Detective Sergeant Cec Johnson. When Paull was interviewed for this book in September 2002, he commented that 'There were some points of similarity' between the Kruger and Wanda cases, but declined to go into too much detail lest he contaminate what remains to this day an ongoing investigation. 'It's easy to pull out some points of comparison and say it could have been [the Wanda Beach killer] but the dissimilar points warn you to back off and not … be in such a hurry to make assumptions.'

Four weeks after the body of Wilhelmina Kruger was discovered in Wollongong, the body of a 27-year-old woman was found 45 kilometres away on the side of the Old Illawarra Road at Menai. On Saturday, 26 February 1966 at about 5.30 p.m., Roy Streeting stopped his truck to change a tyre. When two teenage boys travelling with him decided to investigate the source of a foul smell, they found the mutilated and decomposing body in the bush on the western side of the road.

Detectives identified the woman as Annya Dowlingkoa, born in Perth as Elizabeth Anne Dowling. When her body was found, Dowlingkoa was wearing a gold wedding ring, gold oblong-shaped wristlet watch, green, blue-and-white chequered woollen shirt and long-sleeved red jumper. A black-and-white photograph of a small boy lay beside her body. Despite efforts by investigating police, relatives of the dead woman could not be found and no husband came forward. The identity of the boy in the photograph was never revealed.

Annya Dowlingkoa used seven aliases during her lifetime and had a long criminal record; she was first convicted for vagrancy and soliciting men for sex at the age of twelve. She lived in Cooma for a time, working as a waitress and shop assistant, before coming to Sydney, where she lived in Darlinghurst and drifted back into prostitution. On the night of 16 February 1966, Dowlingkoa told friends at the Grosvenor Club in Kings Cross she was going to meet a client at midnight but should not be too long.

At first detectives were reticent to link her death publicly with the 'Piccadilly Murder' (as the murder of Wilhelmina Kruger became known), but the comparisons were obvious. Dowlingkoa had been strangled and stabbed twice in the chest and, as was the case with the Kruger murder, sexual assault could not be conclusively determined. Interestingly, Dowlingkoa's body remained hidden for several days until it was dragged closer to the highway so it could be discovered. It appeared that, as with the Kruger murder, the killer wanted his handiwork discovered. Detective Sergeant Ron Hinchy of Sydney CIB was placed in charge of the investigation but he quickly called in Detective Sergeant Lendrum of Sydney CIB, who was investigating the Kruger murder.

Detectives investigating Dowlingkoa's murder made little progress because they found it difficult to trace and obtain information from her associates in the Sydney sex industry. Police determined that this was why Dowlingkoa was not reported missing in the ten days between her last appointment and when her body was found. Not surprisingly, despite police appeals, the man with whom she had the midnight appointment did not come forward. Wollongong detectives interviewed local shopkeepers, café owners, hotel managers and motel owners in Wollongong to determine if Dowlingkoa was known there and possibly heading there when she was murdered, but no one knew of her. Or did the murderer live in the region, leaving the body on the side of the Old Illawarra Road on his way back to Wollongong?

On 19 May 1966, police posted a $10,000 reward for information leading to the arrest of the person/s responsible for the deaths of Wilhelmina Kruger and Annya Dowlingkoa. As police wanted a quick resolution to the case and knowing the avalanche of information that followed the record $20,000 reward for information on the Wanda Beach murders, the reward for the Kruger and Dowlingkoa murders was made valid for only twelve months. The Kruger investigation alone would interview over 5000 people. In September 1966, Wollongong coroner James Towns presided over the coronial inquest into the murder of Wilhelmina Kruger. At the time of the inquest, Kruger's de facto husband was in jail for failing to provide child support to his ex-wife; Albert Kruger passed away the week before the inquest started, thereby denying detectives the chance to cross-examine him regarding his wife's relationships. The coronial inquest revealed that Kruger had relationships with a number of men during and after her marriage and had formed an association with a man named Wakefield while Albert Kruger was in hospital in Broken Hill; she subsequently left her husband for Wakefield, who in turn left her. Maurice Cowden, the superintendent of the Piccadilly Arcade, stated that after Kruger moved to Wollongong, Wakefield visited her at work one day. Cowden had met

Wakefield with Kruger, whom he knew quite well, near the cleaners' rooms at the Gladstone Avenue level of the arcade.

A report in the *Illawarra Mercury* on 31 September 1966 claimed that Wilhelmina Kruger formed a number of 'associations' with different men, several of whom knew her working routine at the Piccadilly Arcade. As was the case with Annya Dowlingkoa, the sexual history of Wilhelmina Kruger was only important to the police to help identify potential murder suspects. The respective pasts of both women provided some useful information, but not enough to lead to a conviction.

In a bizarre twist to the investigation, Detective Boyd told the court that on 6 February in the course of general inquiries in the Wollongong area, a man giving his name as Kenneth Garry Munewoe gave information regarding the Kruger murder. Munewoe told Boyd that he was sitting in a car with his girlfriend in Railway Square, near the Piccadilly Arcade, between 2.30 and 3.00 on the morning of Kruger's murder. He said that during this time he saw a utility truck like the one police were looking for parked opposite the drive-in entrance to the Piccadilly Arcade. He also provided a description of a man who got out of the utility. Munewoe gave his address as 42 Gladstone Street, Wollongong, and his date of birth as 6 March 1944, which made him almost twenty-two years old at the time. When police tried to follow up this lead, they discovered that not only had a Kenneth Garry Munewoe never lived in Gladstone Street, 'extensive inquiries' could not locate him in the greater Wollongong area.

Coroner James Towns later handed down an open finding in both the Kruger and Dowlingkoa inquests, bringing to four the number of unsolved sex murders in the 13-month period between January 1965 and February 1966. Many senior detectives now believed that the crimes were indeed related. The four murders were characterised as frenzied assaults using a knife as the primary murder weapon, and in each case no real effort was made to hide the bodies — even in the Wanda Beach case, the two girls were only partially buried. There was now strong reason to believe that detectives had a 'multiple murderer' on their hands.

The term 'serial killer' had not even been invented yet.

CHAPTER 11

CAT AND MOUSE[1]

'The next time you come down to see him, young Alan has something for you.'

The father of convicted murderer Alan Bassett speaking to former Detective Sergeant Cec Johnson in the late 1970s[2]

This chapter tells the story of two men: the man considered by some to be the chief suspect in the deaths of Christine Sharrock and Marianne Schmidt, and the detective who held this belief until the day he died. It is the story of Alan Bassett, a convicted murderer who spent almost thirty years in prison for a sex murder not related to the Wanda crime, and of Cec Johnson, a detective sergeant who worked on the Wanda investigation in the 1960s and pursued a confession from Bassett for decades after the crime. Alan Bassett and Cec Johnson's fourteen-year interaction became well known in police circles, adding to the sense of mystery surrounding the Wanda case. Bassett has continued to profess his innocence of the Wanda crime, and Johnson's failure to credibly link Bassett to the crime hounded Johnson until his death in 1980.

On Monday, 13 June 1966, the *Illawarra Mercury* reported that 'a 21-year-old man was charged in Wollongong Court yesterday with the murder of a Gwynneville girl. He is Alan Raymond Bassett … a fitter and turner of Graham Street, Unanderra.'

The previous Saturday morning at 6.45, the naked body of the young woman, partially covered by a skirt, was found by a local couple on the side of the Mount Ousley [Bypass] Road. The couple originally thought the body was a dressmaker's dummy but as they moved closer saw a trail of clothes leading from the roadway to where the body lay in clear view of passing traffic, just 15 yards from the edge of the road.

The victim, nineteen-year-old Carolyn May Orphin, had already been reported missing by her parents.[3] On Friday, 10 June, Orphin, a punch card operator at the computer room of the Port Kembla Steelworks, met several girlfriends at the Charles Hotel, Fairy Meadow. When the hotel closed at 10.30 p.m., some of the girls continued on to a 'go-go dance' at the Ironworkers' Building near the Jubilee Bridge landmark. There were between 130 and 150 people at the dance that night and the girls were soon dancing with a group of men they did not know. Several people later reported seeing Orphin leave the dance in the company of a young man in a light-coloured Mini Minor sometime between 11.30 p.m. and midnight.

When Orphin's body was found the following morning, her hands were tied behind her back with a stocking and piece of cloth; another stocking and elastic were tied around her throat. A large bloodstained sandstone rock lay beside her and she had suffered a shocking head injury.

Police later linked a car parked in Fairy Street, the entrance to Gipps Street where the girl lived, to the car Orphin was seen getting into at the Ironworkers' Building. A young man was taken into Wollongong Police station on Monday, 13 June and identified in a police line-up by one of Orphin's girlfriends who had accompanied her to the dance. By talking to several witnesses at the dance, police were quickly able to name the man as Alan Bassett of Wollongong. Later that morning, Bassett's car was found parked in his father's service station in Keira Street, Wollongong. Although the car had been cleaned and washed, police found bloodstains, hairs and a woman's palm print inside the grey Mini Minor.

Bassett was questioned by Detective Sergeant Phil Arantz under the supervision of Detective Inspector Lendrum, who was leading the investigation as well as the unsolved Kruger and Dowlingkoa cases. At first, Bassett denied meeting Orphin on the previous Friday. He had gone to the Crown Hotel that night, he told the detectives, but had left at 8.30 p.m. From there he went to the Cabbage Tree Hotel, also at Fairy Meadow, where he stayed until 10.00 p.m. before driving into Wollongong in his car. Bassett told the detectives he was intoxicated at the time and returned home after taking a girl he met in the street for a drive down to North Beach.

In an understated piece of theatre, Arantz produced the piece of cloth that was used to tie Carolyn Orphin's hands behind her back: the effect was immediate. 'Can we scrap this and start again?', Bassett stuttered. The young man paused and then said, 'I did do it'.

Bassett then gave the detectives his version of the murder.[4] Bassett and several other young men went to the dance at the Ironworkers' Building on Friday night after drinking at the Cabbage Tree Hotel. He and Carolyn Orphin danced for 'quite a while' before leaving the dance together; Bassett then drove to a street near her home where they sat in the back of the small car, talking and kissing.

'I don't know', Bassett told Arantz. 'Something just came over me. Everything happened from there.' While they were sitting in the back seat, Bassett took a piece of cloth from his car and tied the girl's hands behind her back. He then started the car and drove to 'the scene where it happened'. He did not know what the time was at this stage, he said, because his watch had stopped.

The girl did not struggle, Bassett said. 'Did she scream?', Arantz asked. 'She did once, that's all.'

'What happened when you pulled up at Mount Ousley [By-pass] Road?' 'I just stripped her and had intercourse with her.' He again made a point of telling the detectives that the girl did not struggle, but contradictorily revealed that he removed the girl's stockings and tied one around her wrists because the cloth he used was becoming loose. 'What did she say?', Arantz prodded.

'She asked me where I was going to drop her. She cried for a while and then she didn't.'

After raping her, Bassett put a stocking around her neck and strangled her; he told Arantz he did not know whether she was conscious when he pulled her out of his car. 'I sort of dragged her up the bank … I just dragged her and dropped her. She seemed still alive.'

Bassett then admitted that he was (also) naked when he dragged the girl's naked body onto an embankment near Mount Ousley [By-pass] Road in the early hours of Saturday morning. Bassett told Arantz that although it was almost winter, he did not put his clothes on until he got back into his car. When asked why he did this, Bassett said he did not want to get dirt on his clothes. Arantz pursued this point: 'You were completely naked when you took the girl's body onto the embankment?'.

'Yes.' An eyewitness in the Wanda Beach case claimed to have seen a naked man walk out of the dunes on the afternoon of the murders, and it had been speculated within police circles that a possible *modus operandi* of the Wanda Beach killer was to commit the murder while naked, thereby leaving no physical evidence at the crime scene.

Arantz probed further. Did Orphin tell him she was a virgin? No, she did not. Did Bassett realise Orphin was menstruating at the time of her death? No, he did not. When police found the girl's dead body, they saw that the elastic strap of her sanitary belt had been tightly wrapped around her neck and used to strangle her. When questioned about the girl's clothing, Bassett said the brassiere straps were broken because Orphin had given him permission to break them to get them off. In reality, Orphin's clothing was ripped off and she was raped in what was described as a 'frenzied attack'.

'When did you drop the rock on her?', Arantz asked. 'After I finished dressing.'

When asked why he did this, Bassett replied: 'I dropped a rock on her head to just knock her out. She was still gurgling and seemed alive.' The understatement of Bassett's confession was shocking: Carolyn Orphin suffered a massive injury to the side of her head. Two bloodstained pieces of the same rock, matted with blood, hair and skin tissue, were found lying beside the girl's body. One of the rocks was the size of a football and the combined weight of the two pieces was a staggering 42 pounds. Bassett also admitted to 'placing his knee' on Orphin's stomach to see if she was still alive.

Bassett stole $6.00 from the dead girl's purse before driving home and going to bed. Bassett told Arantz that he thought Orphin had told him her first name but he could not remember it.

The Wollongong Government Medical Officer, Doctor EM Diment, examined Bassett and noted that he was a 'calm young man, composed and self-assured'. Bassett's pulse rate was recorded as a steady sixty-eight beats per minute and no 'nervous abnormalities' were apparent. Bassett was charged with the murder of Carolyn Orphin at 7.30 p.m.

The following day when local detectives tried to take Bassett into the Wollongong courthouse, they found their passage blocked by a throng of people and had to take their prisoner via a back entrance. The brownhaired young man wore a sports shirt, grey corduroy trousers and suede shoes. When asked if he wanted to apply for bail, Bassett replied, 'I haven't been told anything about it'. Bassett asked to speak to his father but the local sergeant told the court that Bassett's father had gone to Sydney and could not be contacted. Legal aid was arranged and Bassett was remanded in custody until 22 June.

The callousness and senselessness of Carolyn Orphin's murder shocked the Wollongong community and devastated her family. The burial service for the young woman was held in Fairy Meadow on Thursday, 16 June before she was buried at Lakeside Memorial Park. That day's *Illawarra Mercury* reported:

> *Many young people, friends of the murdered girl, were among the mourners … When Mrs Orphin arrived at the church, she was so distressed and had to be assisted from the car by other members of the family. Mr Orphin tried hard to maintain composure. (Carolyn's brother) John and his fiancée were helped from the service.*

Several police who had played an important role in capturing the young man accused of the murder also attended the service.

Alan Bassett stood trial in the Supreme Court in Wollongong on Monday, 25 July 1966, with Mr Justice Collins presiding.[5] Bassett pleaded not guilty to the charge of murder despite the fact that the Crown read a verbatim account of the police interview in which Bassett admitted to stripping, raping and murdering the defenceless girl. Bassett's father sat silently at the back of the Court as the Crown put forward its case. An unusual feature of the trial, which lasted barely two days, was that not one of the thirty or more Crown witnesses was cross-examined, and neither council for the accused nor the Crown made a final address to the jury. The evidence spoke for itself.

Doctor Diment undertook a post-mortem examination of Carolyn Orphin and determined that she died from a fractured skull, with strangulation as a secondary cause. Her neck showed four rope-burns caused by the stocking and sanitary belt used to strangle her. Her body was extensively cut and bruised on her arms and legs, contradicting Bassett's claim that she did not struggle as he had intercourse with and strangled her. The girl fought for her life in the confined spaces of the Mini Minor but Bassett was a fit young man and Orphin's hands were tied behind her back. Orphin's internal injuries were consistent with a knee being pressed into her stomach. There was also evidence of internal damage to her sexual organs and external injuries to her breasts.

A naval rating from HMAS *Albatross* in Nowra gave evidence that he walked past Bassett's Mini Minor parked on the side of the Mount Ousley [By-pass] Road at 3.30 a.m. on the morning of the murder as he hitchhiked home from a party in Sydney. Although he passed within an arm's length of the car, the naval rating could not see inside it because the windows were fogged. One can only speculate what might have happened had the rating knocked on the door of the car, or had Bassett realised he was so close to being interrupted in his murderous act. The next day when the body was discovered, the naval rating contacted police and gave a description of the car.

A number of Bassett's friends told the court that he behaved normally in the hours after the murder on Saturday, 11 June. Bassett picked up some friends and watched a local rugby league match and had a couple of beers at a local pub. Some had known Bassett for two years, others for just over six months. One of Bassett's mates asked him if he was planning to take the girl (he met at the dance on Friday night) out that night?

'No', Bassett said matter-of-factly. 'She's going out with a few of her girlfriends.'

'What's the name of that girl?', another one asked. 'Oh, I forget', was Bassett's reply.

'Where does she live?', they asked.

'In Market Street.' Bassett gave no outward indication that anything was wrong.

One of Bassett's friends who was with him at the dance at the Ironworkers' Building told the Court that he saw Orphin and Bassett sitting together in Bassett's grey Mini Minor outside the club shortly after midnight. On Sunday, 12 June, Bassett's friend recognised the girl from her photograph in the *Sun-Herald*.

Another friend questioned Bassett about washing his car on the day after the murder. 'I was washing the mud off it', Bassett told him.

'Did you say *blood*?', the friend asked. 'No, mud', Bassett repeated.

'Are you the Wanda Beach murderer?', the friend said jokingly. 'Did you dye your hair?' Bassett appeared upset by this suggestion, despite his friend reassuring him it was a joke. This question concerning his hair colour shows how entrenched the image of the suspect was in the community: the teenagers knew that the chief Wanda suspect was a blond 'surfie' type (although this original description provided by seven-year-old Wolfgang Schmidt may have been incorrect, and dark-haired men were also on the list of suspects).

Mr Justice Collins instructed the jury in Bassett's trial that it would have little difficulty in deciding whether Bassett caused the girl's death. The definition of murder — 'with reckless indifference to human life' — was also very clear. The jury deliberated for only sixteen minutes before pronouncing Alan Bassett guilty of the murder of Carolyn Orphin.

In a statement from the dock before he was sentenced,

Bassett told the jury:

> *It's very hard for me to try and explain things. I didn't realise what I was doing at the time of the crime. Something must have come over me and I can't really describe things until further tests have been done on me. I certainly did not intend to kill any girl or any person or any such like. I'd like to ask for a plea of manslaughter, as I don't think it's outright murder. I just ask for your help in my case.*[6]

When Alan Bassett was sentenced to life imprisonment, he showed no emotion and was led from the dock.

Detective Sergeant Keith Paull, who was at this stage in charge of the Wanda Beach murder investigation, was making inquiries into the mutilation murder of Wilhelmina Kruger and was drawn to Alan Bassett's case. Although Carolyn Orphin's body was not mutilated with a knife, there were some striking similarities between the murders of Kruger and Orphin:

- both women were murdered on Saturday mornings;
- both murders occurred on holiday weekends;
- both bodies were left partially naked and in close view of the public;
- both women were strangled and battered;
- the sexual organs and breasts of both women suffered injuries;
- both women suffered an injury consistent with being kneed with considerable force;
- both women lived in Gwynneville, although there is no evidence that Bassett knew either woman before the day he killed Orphin; and

- Kruger was murdered in an arcade close to the Ironworkers' Building where Orphin met Bassett.

The coronial inquest into the death of Wilhelmina Kruger began on 29 September 1966, nine days after Alan Bassett was found guilty of the murder of Carolyn Orphin. At the inquest Doctor Diment, who performed the autopsies on both women, gave evidence that there were:

very many similarities between the two murders, most noticeably the attacks on the sexual organs and breasts of the two women and the fact that both were manually strangled. In both cases, marks which could have been made by teeth were found on the two women.[7]

Not all detectives were as sure. Detective Sergeant Paull told the court that similarities between the deaths of Wilhelmina Kruger and Carolyn Orphin did not necessarily link the crimes together: 'It was a fact that in various crimes there were areas of similarity with complete disassociation of the crimes'.[8] But it did not take a great leap for many detectives working on the unsolved Wanda case to draw similarities between Bassett's crime and the deaths of Christine Sharrock and Marianne Schmidt eighteen months earlier.

Detective Sergeant Arantz, who had built up a good rapport with Bassett, was asked by Sydney police to question the 21-year-old about the Wanda Beach murders. Police running sheets regarding Bassett's interview have been suppressed because they are part of an ongoing investigation but it could be assumed that Bassett was considered a suspect for not only the Wanda Beach murders, but also the murders of Wilhelmina Kruger and Annya Dowlingkoa — when interviewed for this book, friends of Bassett from the 1960s confirmed that Wollongong police reinterviewed them regarding the unsolved murders of Kruger and Dowlingkoa. Inquiries were made at Bassett's place of work regarding his movements on the day Christine Sharrock and Marianne Schmidt were killed. The daily record of employee attendance, however, was only used to compile weekly records of hours clocked up and had been destroyed. The record of the week ending 15 January 1965 showed that Bassett received his full pay for the week, indicating he was present at work on the day of the Wanda Beach murders. The police argued that Bassett may have taken the day off work and would still have received his full week's wage because of accrued sick leave — there was no record of sick days kept by the company to verify this theory.

Police obtained a statement from the manager of the company who, although on holidays at the time, had called into the factory about 8.00 a.m. that day and felt sure that all employees were present, including Bassett.

Although Bassett denied any involvement when interviewed on a number of occasions concerning the Wanda, Kruger and Dowlingkoa crimes, investigating police released the following statement to the press in 1972:

> *Since his [Bassett's] conviction and sentence, inquiries were made into his movements over the years to 1966 — including the period of the Wanda Beach murders in 1965. These inquiries suggest he had been to Cronulla about the time of the Wanda Beach murders.*[9]

A résumé of the Wanda Beach investigation prepared by Detective Sergeant Cec Johnson in January 1973 named Bassett as a prime suspect; six other possible suspects were described but Bassett was the only one named:

Bassett is at present serving a life sentence for the murder of the girl ORPHIN … The reason why Bassett is considered a suspect is because of the vicious way in which he hit the girl Orphin and other similarity in the crimes compared to Mrs Kruger, and the other murders. However, Bassett did not use a knife to murder the girl Orphin as was used in the other murders.

Who is Alan Bassett and why have detectives reviewing the unsolved Wanda case consistently alluded to him, if not by name as the murderer, then as a person of continued interest?

Several men who knew Bassett in the mid-1960s were interviewed for this book in December 2002 and, while wishing to remain anonymous, were able to provide information about Bassett's life prior to Orphin's murder.

Alan Bassett was born in England on 3 May 1945. In 1966 he was a single man living with his parents. One man who knew Bassett in the mid 1960s said:

He was a friend of a mate of ours who met him at Tech … He seemed like a normal guy, but I think he lived a couple of different lives. We'd hang out at the beach and have a couple of beers at a hotel and go home, but he'd stay out with another circle of friends that we never met.

Bassett was known to Wollongong police during his teenage years, so his father was very protective of him, says another friend:

We all used to go to Queensland and surf … But his old man never let Bassett go away with us. There was no inkling that he was violent. He was a quiet, shy sort of guy. It just goes to show that you don't really know people, do you?

The young men who gave evidence against Alan Bassett never really knew much about him or his background. 'I wasn't even game to look at him at the trial', admits one of the men who vaguely knew Bassett all those years ago. When asked if there was a culture at the time concerning knives, the man said: 'No, never. No one had knives in those days, unlike today'. Mindful of the times when it was sociably acceptable to drink and drive, he added, 'The only weapon we ever had in our hands was a schooner glass.'

The night before he was charged with Carolyn Orphin's murder, Bassett was at a friend's home, sitting quietly with his friend's mother while he waited for his mate to come home from the football. But there was more to this quiet young man than first met the eye. After he was charged with Orphin's murder, Bassett was diagnosed with schizophrenia, an often misunderstood mental illness that was particularly stigmatised and mistreated during the 1960s. Not a lot was known then about the mental disorder that today affects, in varying degrees, one in 100 people as either a brief episode in their lives or a long-lasting condition.

Researchers now know that schizophrenia is the name given to a group of mental disorders in which a person may suffer a variety of symptoms including thought disorder, delusions, hallucinations, withdrawal, abnormal emotions, loss of motivation and denial (or lack of insight). Schizophrenia does not refer to any form of mental retardation or split personality, as most commonly misrepresented in the media. While there is no scientific evidence for a single cause of schizophrenia, the onset of the disease can be influenced by genetic, biochemical, environmental and relational factors. As yet, there is no cure for schizophrenia but the symptoms can be effectively controlled through medication, psychotherapy and social and behavioural management.

Schizophrenia is more likely to develop in adolescents and young adults during stressful periods of transition such as puberty, changes to family situations, the move to tertiary education or joining the workforce, but symptoms are also known to develop in middle-aged and elderly people. The onset of symptoms can be rapid, with sudden changes in behaviour over several weeks; or slow, with a gradual deterioration of the personality over a long period.

After his trial, Alan Bassett was assessed and placed in Morisset Psychiatric Hospital, near Newcastle in New South Wales. Police investigating the unsolved deaths of Christine Sharrock, Marianne Schmidt, Wilhelmina Kruger and Annya Dowlingkoa continued to focus their attention on him, particularly Detective Sergeant Cec Johnson, who had been involved in the Wanda case from the early days of the investigation. What followed is part reality, part coincidence wrapped in assumption and myth.

Don Jones, a former colleague and close friend of Johnson, was interviewed for this book in November 2002 and stated:

> *There is no doubt in the world that Cec Johnson went to his grave believing Alan Bassett was the Wanda Beach murderer … Cec went and saw a police psychologist about his theory … [who] recommended that Cec retire from the force because he was becoming paranoid about the case.*

Johnson left the police force in the mid-1970s and retired to the north coast of New South Wales, working as a doorman at a local leagues club, but the Wanda case continued to haunt him.

'Every six months or so, Cec would go down and visit Bassett in Morisset and ask him if he wanted to confess to the murders', Jones recalls. No doubt Bassett enjoyed the attention, giving Johnson just enough information to keep him coming back time and time again. But when it came to the crunch, Bassett would make no formal admission to being involved in the Wanda Beach murders, nor the deaths of Wilhelmina Kruger and Annya Dowlingkoa. Psychologists now believe that offenders often talk to investigators about crimes they may or may not have been involved in as a way to validate their lives — and their crimes. The problem remains that some offenders have been lying all their lives to cover their tracks and are adept at showing different people — family, friends and investigating police — different masks. In Bassett's case, there was also the issue of his schizophrenia and how much it impacted on what he was telling Johnson.

According to those who knew him, Cec Johnson was a personable man with a good sense of humour and a quiet, gentlemanly manner.[10] He knew he had no physical evidence to link Bassett to the Wanda Beach murders but something about the young man bothered him. Bassett's grey Mini Minor would have been easily hidden on one of the many tracks behind Wanda Beach. Then there was the issue of alcohol: the autopsy on Christine Sharrock suggested she had consumed alcohol before she died; Bassett was under the influence of alcohol when he murdered Carolyn Orphin. Was alcohol a trigger of his violent behaviour? Lastly, Bassett's family even began to doubt his innocence — in 1975, Bassett's father secretly blocked his son's parole.

Over the course of several years, Johnson became well known to Bassett and his family and gained their confidence and respect by not violating the trust placed in him or being overly judgmental about Bassett's crime. After one trip to Morisset, Bassett's father rang Johnson and told him: 'The next time you come down to see him, young Alan's got something for you'. At their next meeting, Bassett presented

Johnson with a painting he had done — a blazing bushfire scene, 'bloody awful from an artistic point of view' according to Johnson. But he took it away. Some time later, in early 1975, Johnson hung the painting in his Tweed Heads home. He was showing it to a visiting police colleague from Sydney when he appeared to notice, almost magically, clues to several unsolved murders in the bush scene — the body of a partially clothed woman lying in the scrub; the face of a man etched into the side of a tree-stump (the murderer?). Johnson became convinced that not only did he recognise a scene from the Wanda Beach murders — 'something only the murderer would know', he told Don Jones (although what this evidence was remains unclear) — but there were 'clues' to at least two other unsolved crimes, possibly those of Wilhelmina Kruger and Annya Dowlingkoa.

Johnson immediately went to the press with his theory and appeared on current affairs programs to make a compelling case that the identity of the Wanda Beach murderer had finally been revealed.

Then, unexpectedly, in the late 1970s, Bassett's father went on television, his back to the camera to hide his appearance, to state his belief that his son should never be released from prison. The *Mike Walsh Show*, shown nationally at midday, was predominantly a light-entertainment vehicle but did tackle the political issues of the day and offered viewers the immediacy of access to breaking news stories. On the day Bassett's father appeared on the program, Brian Bury was sitting in Mike Walsh's compere chair. Bury sat stone-faced as Mr Bassett, with voice wavering, told the Australian public that he believed his son was the Wanda Beach murderer. So convinced was Cec Johnson of Bassett's guilt that he planned to write a book about the Wanda case but, tragically, was killed in a pedestrian accident in 1980 before it could be finished. After Johnson's death, his theories concerning

Bassett became part of police subculture, with many detectives content to believe that the Wanda Beach murderer was safely behind bars.

But not everyone shared these thoughts. 'I didn't agree with Cec Johnson, even though I knew him as a fine man', says former colleague Keith Paull. 'It would be [a] poor investigation if we all thought the same when it was an open inquiry and so, one had to respect other opinions.' Many also felt that Johnson's closeness to his suspect had led to tunnel vision about the Wanda case, and investigators understood that knowing a suspect too well can lead to a subconscious effort to make the suspect fit the crime. It is also possible to skew an investigation towards a particular suspect, as happened in the notorious Harry Blackburn case in New South Wales in 1990 (see Chapter 12).

In October 1986 Alan Bassett made headlines of his own when the press revealed that he had been granted unescorted day release from Morisset Psychiatric Hospital on three occasions during a three-month period. The minister for corrective services confirmed at a press conference on 22 October 1986 that the decision to allow Bassett unescorted day leave was made by 'experienced hospital staff', who 'decided that this particular inmate, after twenty years, should be allowed some limited time, unsupervised, in the community'.

A *Sydney Morning Herald* article on 22 October 1986 quoted the opposition spokesman for corrective services as claiming that officials at Morisset Psychiatric Hospital had also recommended that Bassett be released to a nearby caravan park unsupervised for three months. The spokesman stated:

> *Bassett's release highlighted the need to return all dangerous psychiatric prisoners to maximum security*

prisons … If doctors have decided a psychiatric prisoner is sane enough to be allowed out of hospital, he should be returned to prison to serve the rest of his sentence.

Bassett was allegedly released from Morisset to attend a twenty-first birthday party but staff at the hospital filed an official report to the health minister that stated Bassett had returned from his leave with photographs he had taken of several young women. This prompted Bassett's father, who refused to give his first name or reveal where he was now living, to state in the press that he had given up trying to protect the public from his son, whom he still firmly believed to be the Wanda Beach murderer. In a *Daily Mirror* interview on 24 October 1986, Bassett's father said: 'When I stopped his parole eleven years ago, there was a general public outcry. The necks I was trying to save did not appreciate it, so why should I try again?'

In April 1995, almost thirty years after he was convicted of raping and murdering Carolyn Orphin, Alan Bassett was released into the custody of the NSW Health Department and placed in the care of a residential support service. Changes to the NSW *Mental Health Act* in the 1990s meant that 'forensic clients' such as Bassett, who were deemed to be no longer under the influence of their illness, were released into a halfway house and integrated back into the community.

Alan Raymond Bassett is in regular contact with police — as part of his probation and parole he must notify police of any change of address and his case is regularly reviewed by a community mental health team — and continues to profess his innocence of any crime other than the one for which he was convicted in 1966.

CHAPTER 12
AUSTRALIAN PSYCHE[1]

'Perhaps the cosmos likes to strew coincidences around the rim of the funnel into which large events are converging.'

Norman Mailer[2]

As time moved on and the Wanda Beach murder remained unresolved, the murderer took on the spectre of a national ghost. In the late 1960s, parents did not allow their children out of their sight, especially while at the beach. The unknown killer became the stuff nightmares were made of, disturbing the sleep of children and adults alike. If the act of madness at Wanda was not enough, then the disappearance of three children from a South Australian beach twelve months later would leave a permanent scar on the national psyche.

The details surrounding the unsolved case of the missing Beaumont children still hold a macabre fascination for many Australians, particularly those who grew up in the 1960s. Some of the facts have become clouded over time — the countless theories concerning the possible fate of the children have attained urban myth status — but some sinister parallels can be drawn between the disappearance of the Beaumonts and the deaths of Christine Sharrock and Marianne Schmidt at Wanda Beach.

On Wednesday, 26 January 1966, the three children of Jim and Nancy Beaumont — nine-year-old Jane, seven-year-old Arnna and four-year-old Grant — asked their parents if they could go to Glenelg Beach for a swim. Jim Beaumont had to work that day, but the temperature was expected to top 100 degrees on the old Fahrenheit scale and the children were persistent. Finally their mother allowed them to make the short bus trip from their home suburb of Somerton Park to Glenelg if they promised to come home on the midday bus. Nancy Beaumont gave the children eight shillings and sixpence to buy some pasties for lunch, telling them to bring one home for her.

The Beaumont children left their home at 10.00 a.m. and caught a bus ten minutes later from the corner of Diagonal Road and Peterson Street, just 100 metres from their home. The bus driver remembered seeing the children get off the bus at Mosely Street, just a short walk from the beach, the eldest girl carrying a paperback copy of *Little Women* under her arm.

At 11.00 a.m., a woman noticed the children playing under the sprinkler on the lawn on the adjoining Colley Reserve. Fifteen minutes later, a man wearing a blue swimming costume had joined the three children; the children were flicking him with their towels and the four were playing under the water. At about 11.45 Jane, Arnna and Grant went into a milk bar on Jetty Street and bought some pasties and a pie. Although Nancy Beaumont had given her eldest daughter some coins to buy lunch, Jane paid for the food with a £1 note.

Another woman, who was sitting on a park bench with her husband and ten-year-old granddaughter, noticed the man and three children return to the reserve area around midday. The man later approached the group and asked if they had seen anyone going through his belongings, as some money was missing. They told him they had not, and he returned to the children. They all seemed friendly towards the man, the woman later told detectives. Soon after, the man started dressing the children for their trip home.

Witnesses described the man as being in his late thirties or early forties, 5 feet 11 inches, with a thin face and athletic build. His hair was light brown, parted on the side and long at the back. Although he had a fair complexion he was suntanned and generally described as a 'surfie type'. Another woman noticed the man pick up his towel and trousers and walk with the children to the Colley Reserve change rooms at about 12:15 p.m.; there the children waited on a seat for him while he dressed. The group then walked behind the Glenelg Hotel. A local postman who knew the children later told police that he saw the three youngsters (there was no one else with them) walking east along Jetty Road towards Mosely Street, apparently to catch the bus home. The postman could not remember if it was at the start of his round at 1.45 p.m. or at the end at 2.55 p.m., but this proved to be the final sighting of the children.

While her children were at the beach, Nancy Beaumont visited friends but returned home in time to meet the midday bus. When the children did not arrive she was not immediately concerned — and presumed they would be on the two o'clock bus. When the two o'clock bus came and went, she felt she should go and look for them — perhaps they missed the bus and were walking home. But the children could be walking any of four different ways home so she decided to stay and wait for the three o'clock bus.

The children never came home.

When Jim Beaumont arrived home at 3.30 p.m. and was told that the children had not returned from the beach, he immediately took his wife to Glenelg Beach and searched for them. The children were reported missing at 7.30 that night.

By the following day, a massive search for the Beaumont children was underway. There were three plausible theories put forward by police at the time — the children had drowned, they had run away or they had been abducted. The first option was quickly dismissed: it was highly unlikely that the three siblings could drown unnoticed on a crowded beach, and the children's belongings had not been found. The second explanation defied logic: these were kids from a happy family heading off for a day at the beach. The third theory also had its detractors: multiple abductions, especially three children from the same family, were almost unheard of.

The coastline north and south of Glenelg Beach was searched but no trace of the children or their belongings was found. Hundreds of Adelaide citizens joined the search, as did members of the Suburban Taxi Service after it was discovered that Jim Beaumont was a former ownerdriver. In the days following her children's disappearance, Nancy Beaumont was sedated and comforted by friends. Jim Beaumont visited the Glenelg police station twice daily, waiting for the news that would never come of his children's fate.

On 31 January, five days after his children's disappearance, Jim Beaumont went on national television to appeal to the public for any information that would lead to their return. 'I hope whoever is holding my children will return them', Jim Beaumont said on Adelaide's Channel 7 midday broadcast. While the nation collectively held its breath for the safe return of the children, the public feeling was that the three Beaumont children were most likely already dead, buried in an unmarked grave.

Police were swamped with erroneous leads. People claimed they had seen the children in a car, or 'children who looked like the children' holidaying interstate. A 33-year-old labourer telephoned police and said that a man driving a Holden came to his house in the Adelaide Hills and forced him to fill the Holden's radiator at gunpoint: inside the car were three children matching the description of the

Beaumonts. The man signed a statement to this effect but was later charged with providing a false statement.

On Thursday, 3 February 1966, Nancy Beaumont held a press conference in the garden of her home. 'I can't be stupid and say they're going to come in with a skipping rope', the 38-year-old mother told the press. 'I've got to feel the little things are huddled up somewhere and nobody has found them.' Jane Beaumont was a sensible, mature girl, her mother told the press. 'If the other two were keen to go with someone, Jane would go with them to look after them and wouldn't leave them alone.' Everything that could be done to find the children was done. The day of Nancy Beaumont's press conference, the Patawalonga Boat Haven was searched at low tide: the gates were secured, the lock drained and while divers searched upstream, fifty police cadets waded waist-deep in the sludge. Later, the Adelaide Hills were searched along with the rubbish tip at Marion. People living in seaside suburbs of Adelaide were asked to check stormwater drains and wells. No trace of the children was found.

Sydney detectives investigating the murders of Christine Sharrock and Marianne Schmidt could only have envisaged the remotest link between the Wanda Beach murders and the disappearance of the Beaumont children from Glenelg Beach twelve months later. But the timing and place of the two crimes — in the January school holidays and on a public beach — was uncanny. On closer inspection, there was the most tenuous of connections. One of the prime suspects, the serial pest at Wanda and North Cronulla beaches, said he was from Adelaide. 'I come from Adelaide', the man had told women on the beach, 'I'm on holidays. How about the sex in Sydney?'.[3] Although the description of the Beaumont suspect did not match that of 'The Fat Man' from the Wanda Beach investigation, eyewitness accounts of the man seen propositioning women on the Sydney beaches varied greatly, and the suspect could have changed his appearance in the twelve months that had passed since he was last sighted.

The only connection Sydney police had with the Beaumont case was in March 1966 when retired Detective Inspector Ray 'Gunner' Kelly arrived in Adelaide. Sponsored by a Sydney newspaper, Kelly had been hired as a private detective to investigate the disappearance of the children. The South Australian police were reportedly welcoming and polite but Kelly left after only one day.

The investigation into the disappearance of the Beaumont children stretched the limited resources of the South Australian police to their fullest and eventually had to be scaled down. The only sightings of the children occurred at Glenelg on the day they disappeared. Not a single piece of evidence has been found since.

As was the case with the deaths of Christine Sharrock and Marianne Schmidt, the disappearance (and probable murder) of the three Beaumont children shocked the nation, and the conservative Australian public struggled to come to terms with the crimes. When traditional police methods again failed to produce a satisfactory resolution to the crime, the public placed its faith in more unconventional methods — reckless gossip fuelled by national media exposure and hunches from the well-intentioned that served only to distract police from their investigation. And then came the psychics and charlatans, as the Beaumont investigation quickly took a bizarre turn.

In March 1966, a Dutchman living in Adelaide recommended that Jim and Nancy Beaumont consult Gerard Croiset, a well-known psychic in The Netherlands. Croiset had had some success in solving cases in Europe, especially those concerning missing children. Croiset contacted the Beaumonts in July 1966, stating that the children were buried within half a mile of where they were last sighted. He asked that a film of the area around Glenelg Beach and photographs of the children (but not items of the children's clothing) be sent overseas to him. According to Croiset, the children were 'under the earth in a cave'. Croiset first believed the children had been crawling through a 'tunnel' that had caved in, but a search of coastal stormwater drains proved fruitless.

When a local man, acting of his own volition, found some items while digging in dunes near an oval behind a home for mentally disabled children, Croiset claimed that the children were buried metres from where a straw hat had been found. In September 1966 the dunes were extensively searched but nothing was found. The problem of communicating with someone on the other side of the world was said to be hindering the investigation so, in November, a group of businessmen paid for Croiset to be flown to Adelaide. Croiset quickly became part of a huge media circus, walking Glenelg Beach and talking into a tape recorder while being followed by a trail of spectators.

When a woman contacted Croiset and told him the floor of a food warehouse in Paringa Park — not far from where Jane and Arnna Beaumont attended primary school — had recently been concreted, he claimed the bodies of the three children were buried there. Despite the fact that police had no evidence to substantiate Croiset's claim, this theory took on a life of its own and Croiset eventually backed a plan to excavate the floor. A committee raised $7000 for the specific purpose of ripping up the concrete floor and, in March 1967, this was partially completed. This story became part of Australian urban folklore and it was not until 1996, thirty years after the Beaumont children disappeared, that the warehouse floor was entirely ripped up. No evidence of the children was found.

The disappearance brought out the very worst in

human nature. Anonymous callers abused Jim and Nancy Beaumont for allowing their children to go to the beach unsupervised. Then, there were the poison-pen writers and pranksters. In February 1968 Jim Beaumont received a letter — postmarked Dandenong, Victoria, on 21 February — written in a child's handwriting and signed from 'Jane'. The letter stated that if Jim went to the Dandenong Post Office at 8.50 a.m. on Monday, 26 February, wearing a dark coat and white trousers, the children would be returned to him there. Although the writer of the letter threatened to cancel the arrangement if the police were contacted — and Arnna's name was consistently been misspelled as 'Arna' — Jim Beaumont contacted Detective Sergeant Swaine of the Adelaide Police Department and they decided to keep the appointment.

Jim Beaumont and the Adelaide police conducted the trip to Dandenong in great secrecy and did not notify local Melbourne police of the meeting. The letter, however, was leaked to the press and the *Adelaide News* broke the story the afternoon before the appointment. Local police also learnt of the plan through the press after the publican who owned the Dandenong hotel where Jim Beaumont and Detective Sergeant Swaine were staying became suspicious and contacted the local police. A detective recognised Swaine's name in connection with the Beaumont case and rang the Melbourne *Herald* to inquire if there had been any developments in the case the local police were not aware of. When Jim Beaumont kept his appointment outside the Dandenong Post Office the following morning, two reporters from the *Herald* were watching as events unfolded.

At 9.00 a.m., a postal worker delivered a message to Jim Beaumont; a man had phoned and said that the children would be there shortly. Some time later a telegram was delivered, saying that Grant Beaumont was sick and the children would not be able to come until after lunch. Beaumont waited until 3.00 p.m. but no one showed up. When Beaumont and Swain returned to their hotel they were confronted by journalists from the *Adelaide News*.

Three more letters were sent to the Beaumonts, two from 'Jane' and one signed from 'The Man'. The children had not been returned, the letters stated, because the police had been informed. In 1992 improvements in fingerprint technology allowed police to identify the man who wrote these letters to the Beaumonts: a Victorian man, who was seventeen years old at the time he wrote the letters, told police it had all been a joke. He was charged and jailed for creating a public mischief.

Not knowing the fate of their children ultimately took its toll on Jim and Nancy Beaumont's marriage, the pair divorcing and retreating to the anonymity of private life. The case has remained open all these years, with many alleged sightings of the children — only older — reported to police. Computer–enhanced photographs of what the children might possibly look like as adults were circulated in the mid-1990s; Nancy Beaumont could not bear to look at them.

Sydney journalist Steve Raymond also covered the disappearance of the three Beaumont children, and discussed his experiences and recollections in a May 2003 interview for this book. 'At the time, there was some thought that [the Beaumont case] could be linked to Wanda', he said. Raymond flew to Adelaide to cover the Beaumont case, but again the investigation faltered as 'another unsolved crime burned into the brain'. The Wanda Beach murders, however, stayed with him:

I had read about the success of the first 'crime-stoppers' program in Germany in 1969 and it had stayed in my mind that something wasn't quite right about the Wanda Beach murders … the fact that the case had stalled and was never resolved considering the amount of effort thrown at it.

In 1969 Raymond contacted NSW Police Commissioner Norm Allan and said that he wanted to make a news documentary about the Wanda Beach murders. Raymond recalled:

> *Allan issued a public statement that said that for the first time he had ordered all files and running sheets to be handed over, and I spent the next four months — every spare moment and weekends — in a little room at Cronulla police station going through all the statements … On that basis, I made the program* The Wanda Beach Murders: The Sands Cannot Tell, *putting in all the factual information I had gathered and bringing the original people involved back, to re-enact where they were and what happened on the day [of the murders].*

Raymond brought together Peter Smith, the youth who had discovered the bodies in January 1965; Barry Ezzy, the lifeguard on duty at Wanda that day; the surviving Schmidt children; and the police who first investigated the crime. Together, they attempted to re-create the final events leading up to the deaths of Christine Sharrock and Marianne Schmidt:

> *Mrs Schmidt gave us permission to film the re-enactment in [her] house and in the children's bedrooms … the kids waking up, getting dressed and having breakfast, taking off for the beach. We used look-alikes for the two [murdered] girls. Helmut [Schmidt] was the one person*

who thought [the re-enactment] was wrong. He was very suspicious, for one reason or another. He was not welcoming at all in what we were trying to do. There was no dialogue ... the idea was to trigger the memories of people who might have seen them on the train or at the beach.

The program aired as a Channel 10 news special in late 1969, as Raymond recalled:

It went to air and had a big impact in Sydney ... we took over 400 calls and opened up some new lines of inquiry, but it didn't succeed in bringing anyone [to] trial. I was really optimistic that something would come from it.

Raymond expressed frustration at what he felt was a lack of energy being focused on the Wanda case at the time the program was made, five years after the girls' deaths. More than this, he believed that some of the police who were speaking out publicly about the case were not familiar with the files that he had been given access to. He quickly formed the opinion that, while many policemen had indeed 'lived' the Wanda case, 'some police take on the "celebrated" cases as a career ... [it is as if] they think that as there is no chance of bringing someone to conviction, they can live off the case forever'.

Over time, the Wanda Beach murders passed into Australian subculture, often providing the subtext for Australian criminal fiction. In 1993, authors Stuart Coupe and Julie Ogden edited the best-selling crime anthology *Case Reopened*,[4] which was comprised of noted crime writers' fictional accounts of unsolved crimes. The chapter relating to the Wanda Beach murders was written by Robert

Hood and entitled 'Sandscrawlers'. The following year, plans were underway for Coupe and Ogden, along with noted writers Bob Ellis and David O'Brien, to produce an eight-part TV series that offered hypothetical solutions to notorious unsolved crimes such as the Bogan-Chandler case, the Beaumont case and, of course, Wanda, but nothing came of it. Dave Warner, the former frontman of the 1970s cult Australian band From the Suburbs and now an accomplished author, chose the Wanda Beach murders as a subplot for his second book, *Big Bad Blood*,[5] a fictional account of the Sydney crime scene in the 1960s.

But this was only fiction, and the reality of what happened at Wanda Beach was sobering enough material. In 1993, Bill Jenkins, the former News Ltd crime reporter, published his memoirs, entitled *As Crime Goes By*.[6] Jenkins dedicated a chapter to his coverage of the Wanda Beach murders and nominated Alan Raymond Bassett as the likely murderer. Lawyers acting on Bassett's behalf threatened to sue for defamation but Jenkins died shortly after and Bassett, who was still in Morisset Psychiatric Hospital at the time, did not follow through on this threat.

During the past four decades, a number of theories have been thrown into the public arena concerning the identity of the Wanda Beach murderer. One of the more recent suspects to emerge is convicted paedophile and child killer Derek Ernest Percy. In 1969 Percy was found not guilty on the grounds of insanity for the murder of twelve-year-old Yvonne Elizabeth Tuohy. The young girl was abducted while walking with her friend Shane Spiller (also twelve years old) to Westernport Beach for a picnic. Spiller escaped from Percy and was able to provide a detailed description to police, but was haunted by the young girl's death all his life. With the Victorian Supreme Court reviewing changes to laws relating to people serving indefinite sentences under 'Government Pleasure' rulings, the possibility of Derek Percy being released proved too much for Spiller. In November 2002 the recluse went missing from his New South Wales south coast home and has not been seen since.

In a *Sydney Morning Herald* article by John Silvester, published on 14 June 1998, a prison officer who supervised Derek Percy for ten years described Percy as 'our Hannibal Lecter. He's highly intelligent but you could never get a handle on his real thoughts.' Silvester reported that 'exercise books seized from Percy's cell showed graphic details of plans to commit crimes against children'. The Adult Parole Board of Victoria consistently refused to recommend Percy's release and psychiatrists failed to recommend Percy's removal to a less secure hospital.

Detectives investigating the Tuohy murder linked Derek Percy to not only the deaths of Christine Sharrock and Marianne Schmidt at Wanda Beach, but also the disappearance of the Beaumont children, the murder of Canberra schoolboy Alan Redston in 1966 and the 1968 abduction murders of four-year-old Sydney boy Simon Brook and seven-year-old Linda Stillwell of Melbourne. Percy, who was in the air force at the time of his capture, had alibis for some of the murders but not all. Dick Night, one of the original investigators in the Tuohy case and later Deputy Victorian Police Commissioner, went on record to say he 'believed Percy could have been involved in other murders',[7] and Detective Inspector Paul Sheridan of the Victorian Police confirmed that Percy was being investigated regarding these unsolved crimes.

One of the more fanciful theories, which ended up causing severe embarrassment to the NSW Police, was publicly tabled during the 'Harry Blackburn affair' in 1990. On 24 July 1989, Harry Blackburn, a former NSW Police Superintendent, was publicly arrested in front of a large media gallery and charged with twenty-five offences, many of a sexual nature. Incredibly, just three months later, the police case fell apart and all charges were dropped. Blackburn later won a huge settlement from the NSW Police, with a royal commission formed to inquire into the conduct of the investigating police. According to evidence produced at the royal commission, the original police investigation into Harry Blackburn was based on a 'hunch' by Detective Sergeant Jim Thornthwaite.

Thornthwaite's former superior officer, Detective Chief Superintendent Alfred Peate, declared during the royal commission that Thornthwaite was also obsessed with the Wanda Beach murders. In 1988 — twenty-three years after the Wanda Beach crime — Thornthwaite formed a new theory concerning the murders, based on a report that a local man driving along Captain Cook Drive in Cronulla had, on the day of the murders, seen a man running from the sand dunes covered 'from ankles to nose' in blood.[8] Thornthwaite stated that the car was 'parked off Captain Cook Drive about halfway to Kurnell between noon and 3.00 p.m.', and police wanted to talk to anyone who saw a grey car near the murder site on the afternoon of 11 January 1965.[9]

At the height of the 1990 Blackburn royal commission, Superintendent Peate used a *Sydney Morning Herald* article by Malcolm Brown, published on 22 April 1990, to publicly contradict Thornthwaite's hunch regarding the new Wanda Beach suspect. Peate stated that a major weakness in Thornthwaite's investigation was 'that the informant was a drinker in Sergeant Thornthwaite's local pub. Another was that in order to get a positive identification, Sergeant Thornthwaite … walked the informant past the place where the suspect worked.' Thornthwaite's police career was effectively over.

As a footnote to the Blackburn royal commission,

Superintendent Peate publicly stated that he believed he knew who committed the Wanda Beach murders but he had insufficient evidence to lay charges. Peate retained this view when he was officer-in-charge of the State Intelligence Section of the NSW Police. Although Peate did not reveal the identity of the person he believed was responsible for the Wanda Beach murders, Peate's opinion was indicative of the police subculture that expounded the belief that the killer had been behind bars all those intervening years.

One of the more plausible theories to emerge recently concerns American serial killer Christopher Wilder, who was shot and killed by Massachusetts police in April 1984 after a forty-day murder spree across the United States. Wilder was born in Sydney on 13 March 1945 in the dying months of World War II to an American naval officer and an Australian woman. Wilder's childhood was plagued by illness — he was given last rites at birth and almost drowned at age two; the following year he suffered a series of convulsions while travelling in his family's car and had to be resuscitated.

In 1962 the seventeen-year-old Wilder was, along with several accomplices, charged with the gang rape of a girl on a Sydney beach; Wilder pleaded guilty to the lesser charge of carnal knowledge and was placed on one year's probation and ordered to undertake counselling. The rehabilitation program included therapy and electric shock treatment. Wilder was married at the age of twenty-three but the marriage only lasted a matter of weeks, with his wife complaining of physical and sexual abuse and leaving him after finding pairs of other women's underpants and photographs of naked women in a case in his car.

Christopher Wilder was always one step ahead of the law. In November 1969 he used nude photographs to demand sex from a nurse but she later withdrew the complaint she had made to the police. Moving to Florida in the United States,

Wilder made a good living in construction and electrical contracting. Borrowing heavily, he financed a playboy lifestyle built around racing luxury cars and even constructed a photographic studio in his apartment to pursue his other passions. In March 1971 he was charged with soliciting women to pose for nude photographs but agreed to a lesser plea of disturbing the peace and was fined. He was jailed briefly in October 1977 after threatening to beat a girl if she did not perform oral sex on him and despite admitting to the crime to a court-assigned therapist, he was acquitted. In June 1980 he coerced a girl into his car on the premise of taking her to a modelling job, and then raped her. Wilder again copped the lesser plea, this time of attempted sexual battery, and was given five years' probation and ordered to undergo mandatory counselling. During his therapy sessions, Wilder admitted to suffering from blackouts — possibly a sign of schizophrenia. At the time of the Wanda Beach murders in January 1965, Wilder was aged nineteen and living in Sydney. Although Wilder appeared slightly older than the boy Wolfgang Schmidt allegedly saw walking with his sister before her death, the physical descriptions did match: Wilder, like Wolfgang's 'fat boy', was short, stocky and blond. Could Wilder have been the Wanda Beach murderer?

The chilling events throughout his life must raise the possibility.

On 28 December 1982, during a visit to see his parents in Australia, Wilder allegedly kidnapped two fifteen-year-old girls from a NSW beach and forced them to pose for pornographic photographs. Captured the following day after police traced him through the licence plates of his rented car, Wilder was charged with kidnapping and indecent assault. Incredibly, his family posted $350,000 bail and the court allowed him to return to the United States to meet his car racing commitments. Wilder was due back in Australia for his trial on 3 April 1984 but by that time he was wanted for a series of murders across the United States.

Between 6 February and 14 April 1984 Wilder murdered eight women across seven States — Florida, Texas, Oklahoma, Colorado, California, Indiana and New York. One of his victims was able to talk him out of murdering her in return for assisting him to lure others to their deaths. Another was taken to a motel where she was repeatedly raped and tortured with electric shocks; she was able to escape by locking herself in the bathroom and screaming to draw the attention of motel guests. Eight women were not as fortunate. Wilder's *modus operandi* was always the same: he would approach women and young girls in public places, usually at shopping malls, and inquire about photographing them for modelling purposes. The women would agree to meet him and were then abducted, raped and stabbed or shot to death. Two of his victims' bodies have never been found.

The end came for Christopher Wilder when one of his victims was left for dead after being stabbed outside Rochester, New York; she survived the attack and alerted police to the fact that Wilder, already the focus of a national manhunt, was in the State. With his sixteen-year-old unwilling accomplice in his car, Wilder murdered his final victim near Victor, New York, before inexplicably driving his accomplice to Boston airport and buying her a one-way ticket home to Los Angeles. On 13 April 1984, after attempting to abduct a woman near Beverley, Massachusetts, Wilder was sighted by State troopers at a service station in Colebrook, New Hampshire. After a violent struggle, Wilder was shot dead with his own gun. One of the most gripping manhunts in FBI history, which had unfolded under the scrutiny of the world media, ended.

What made Wilder turn from voyeur and sexual predator

to serial killer will remain unclear. There are countless unsolved crimes and lists of missing persons, especially young women, in both the United States and Australia to suggest that Wilder's murder spree may actually have started earlier than 1982. Here was a charming, self-assured man who surrounded himself with the trappings of a successful business life, but Wilder was also a sociopathic killer who showed little remorse for what he had done to his victims.

Could Christopher Wilder have first indulged his bloodlust at Wanda Beach as a teenager in 1965? Although Wilder's possible association with the Wanda Beach murders has been described as a 'red herring' in the past (there is a seventeen-year gap between the deaths of Christine and Marianne and Wilder's first known murder in the United States), the NSW Police are obviously aware of Wilder's criminal record in this state. However, when contacted for this book, they would neither confirm nor deny that they had investigated Wilder as a Wanda suspect.

The spectre of unsolved murders still haunts society today and the Wanda, Kruger and Dowlingkoa cases remain open. Theories concerning potential suspects — some old, some new — will always be entertained by the police and the public.

CHAPTER 13
ANTIQUITY

'Today, I still stand firm that the girls didn't know their killer. This is what I've always believed. And I never imagined the person responsible being out on the streets. The thought of the Wanda Beach murderer marrying the girl next door, having kids and living happily ever after has never entered into my mind.'

Margaret Kavazos, Christine Sharrock's childhood friend[1]

When Austrian abbot and botanist Gregor Johann Mendel began his research into the inheritance characteristics of garden peas in 1857, he could not have known the impact he would have over a century later on the seemingly unrelated field of forensic criminology. Mendel's experiments in plant genetics led to the formation of his principles of factorial inheritance — the statistical laws governing the transmission of 'unit hereditary factors', which we now call genes. Mendel's groundbreaking work, which was not appreciated until long after his death in 1884, provided the basis for the modern study of genetics and the discovery of DNA. DNA (deoxyribonucleic acid) is found in almost all living cells and is commonly known as a genetic 'fingerprint' that is unique to every individual human (except identical twins, who share the same DNA coding). The advent of DNA coding technology has not only created a powerful tool for examining genetic relationships but has also revolutionised the ways police throughout the world investigate crime. Could this sophisticated technology, now available to a new generation of criminal investigators, finally unlock the mystery of the Wanda Beach murders before the case is forever consigned to history?

While DNA testing is frequently used to determine how particular people are related to each other, such as in paternity suits, it did not take long for law enforcement agencies to realise the impact this process could have on crime investigation. If a tiny amount of biological material, such as a drop of blood or a human hair, is recovered from a crime scene, scientists can extract the DNA and mix it with restriction enzymes. These enzymes cut the long chains of DNA into different lengths according to the individual. Once cut, each person's DNA gives a unique set of different-sized pieces. Therefore, to match or exclude a suspect or victim to DNA recovered from a crime scene, scientists simply compare and contrast the respective cuts of DNA.

The first use of DNA technology in a murder investigation in New South Wales occurred in 1988. On 8 September that year, 21-year-old Janine Balding was kidnapped from the Sutherland railway station carpark by a gang of youths who also stole her car. After being raped by several members of the group, the young woman was bound and gagged before being drowned in a western Sydney dam. DNA technology helped send several young men to jail for the rest of their lives for this crime, but the DNA samples had to be sent overseas for analysis, so the process was very slow. Over time the technology has improved and DNA testing is now standard procedure in ongoing criminal investigations. For example, in January 2003 improved DNA technology allowed NSW detectives to extradite a man from Tasmania and charge him with the murder of a 21-year-old woman twelve years earlier.[2]

DNA testing allows for the possibility of solving current crimes as well as many from the past, as long as recoverable, uncontaminated DNA samples are available. Unfortunately, in cases stretching back to the 1960s such as the Wanda Beach murders, this may not be the case. As former Detective Sergeant Keith Paull said in a September 2002 interview for this book: 'A lot of matters come to light many years after they occur. The passage of time can create matters of importance — if they're not stuffed up along the way!'.

The only physical evidence recovered from the Wanda Beach crime scene in 1965 was the clothing the girls were wearing that day. A sliver of stainless steel, possibly from a knife blade, was also found in the sand some distance away but there was no way of determining whether it was used in the murders. A sperm sample was taken from the body of Marianne Schmidt but the current state of the sample has not been confirmed. The detectives investigating the case in its fifth decade — Detective Inspector Wayne Hayes and Detective Sergeant Carla Tomadini — cannot comment on an ongoing investigation. However, in a letter dated 9 January 2003 Tomadini confirmed that 'DNA technology has not impacted the investigation at this stage'.

While the police would neither confirm nor deny whether Alan Bassett has provided them with a DNA sample, Bassett, in a *Telegraph Mirror* interview in 2000, volunteered to provide a DNA sample to clear his name once and for all. The fact that police have stated that DNA has not impacted the Wanda case could mean one of the following: Bassett has not supplied a sample; Bassett has supplied a sample but it did not match DNA taken from the scene; or DNA from the murderer was not recoverable and therefore DNA testing cannot prove the killer's identity. The failure to lay charges against any 'known person' does mean that the current police investigation has reached a dead end. All cases of unsolved murders within New South Wales remain open.

Why, then, has the Wanda Beach investigation failed to

identify the murderer of Christine Sharrock and Marianne Schmidt? Statistically, it is unlikely that the killer was not known in some way to the police. Even if he was a first-time killer and had not been in trouble with the law, in 94 per cent of cases police possess some information about a suspect before their conviction — an address, a phone number, a licence plate, a description. One of the main reasons the Wanda Beach murder investigation faltered was the volume of incoming information — it simply became too much for the police force to handle. But, in fairness, it must be said that no one in the NSW Police had the experience to process the scope of information, which was unprecedented in NSW criminal history. In the early stages of the investigation, the public provided literally hundreds of leads daily, and police were simply not accustomed to receiving information in this magnitude and manner. There was no way of enabling detectives to collect information in a systematic way and prioritise it. The data recording system police used at the time of the Wanda Beach investigation consisted of each piece of information being written on paper, allocated a reference number and committed to memory. Obviously, there were no personal computers available for compiling and cross-referencing information, which now happens using specifically designed software (national databases now exist that profile convicted murderers, paedophiles and rapists). The volume of information compiled by a case today does not deter detectives and, as Robert Keppel, president of the Institute for Forensics in Seattle, Washington, stated in a 2000 interview, 'the more information you have (today), the more likely you are to succeed'.[3]

Another flaw in the Wanda case involved the examination of the crime scene. The current procedure for conducting shoulder-to-shoulder searches of crime sites, crawling on hands and knees if required, was unheard of in the 1960s.

This procedure was pioneered by the aviation industry in the 1970s with the use of rescue scout teams to recover physical evidence left behind from aircraft crashes. As outlined in Chapter 4, the use of forensic technology at the Wanda Beach crime scene was minimal in 1965, while the sifting of sand around the burial site lacked any technical sophistication. According to Robert Keppel, today the opposite is true: 'Most homicide investigators are overtrained in crime scene processing but no one ever teaches them how to follow leads and investigate them'.[4] If, as some detectives believed, the Wanda Beach murders were connected to the deaths of Wilhelmina Kruger and Annya Dowlingkoa, the police were looking for a serial killer a full decade before technology and research turned this task into a science. Offender profiles composed by psychologists and psychiatrists, now the norm in investigating murder and serial murder crimes, played no part in police investigations in the 1960s. The FBI did not start using psychological profiling until 1974 when they were searching for an unidentified 'repeat murderer' in the greater Seattle area: that killer turned out to be Ted Bundy, the first person referred to as a serial killer, who was responsible for the murder of at least twenty-eight women in three states during the 1970s. As stated in Chapter 4, the closest thing to a psychological profile presented in the Wanda Beach case was supplied by leading forensic psychiatrist Dr John McGeorge, who was quoted in the *Daily Mirror*, on 14 January 1965:

> *This (crime) appears to be an insane, sadistic killing rather than a sex crime. I believe the murderer is a schizophrenic — a late teenager or in his early 20s ... withdrawn, unsociable, peculiar in his mannerisms. The sexual side of the crime is secondary. The killer is young, cunning and given to sudden violence. (He is) suffering a grave, mental disturbance.*

In 1961, American psychologists Samuel Yochelson and Stanton Samenow published a breakthrough study into the criminal mind. The two liberals, who were researching the inherent reasons why people turn to crime, were shocked by their own findings. They found the chief characteristics of the criminal to be 'weaknesses, immaturity, vanity and self delusion'. Criminals are 'hypersensitive to what was said to them … lacked selfdiscipline and were cowards', their greatest fear being the possibility of other people identifying some weakness in them.[5] This profile uncannily matches a number of suspects who later came under the notice of detectives investigating the murders.

Can the current bank of research, then, point detectives in the right direction? Former FBI agent Robert K Ressler is the world's foremost expert on serial killers.[6] Ressler invented the term 'serial killer' and, having interviewed more murderers than anyone else for his book *Whoever Fights Monsters*, identified several characteristics common in the majority of repeat killers. He found that:

- most serial killers are white males under the age of thirty-five;
- most serial killers are the products of dysfunctional families, typified by an unloving mother or an absent father;
- many serial killers are intelligent, but are employed in menial jobs far below their intellectual ability;
- many serial killers suffer from physical ailments or disabilities; and the initial impulse to murder comes during a period of stress; such as the loss of a job or break-up of a relationship.[7]

Professor David Canter, Britain's leading criminal psychologist and profiler, has put forward his 'circle hypothesis', in which criminals, including 'a large percentage of serial killers' live within an area circumscribed by their crimes.[8] Author William Beadle writes that as well as alcohol playing a role in many violent crimes, including serial murder, another common element is theft. Serial killers 'will have engaged in various other forms of crime, the most common being theft (and) sometimes this is carried forward into their murders'.[9]

The theory that each serial killer has a distinctive signature — a psychological calling card — is also a relatively new concept. If the murders of Christine Sharrock, Marianne Schmidt, Wilhelmina Kruger and Annya Dowlingkoa are indeed linked, the common thread would be sexual assault after the victims' deaths, the use of a knife, the exposed or partially exposed condition of the bodies and the probable use of a car to escape the crime scene. While serial killers may have an ideal victim type and preferred method of murder, this does not mean the victim or opportunity is always presented. This may explain the seemingly unrelated nature of the victims — naïve teenagers, elderly cleaning woman and experienced prostitute; and the varied crime scenes — desolate beach, empty car park and outer-Sydney roadway.

And what if the Wanda Beach murderer was not insane? The pathological murderer must also kill and keep on killing. Robert Keppel says, 'In a population of murders the repeat murderer is one who is rare compared to those who commit single victim crimes'.[10] Throw in the sexual assault motive for the deaths of these four women, and this murderer would have been even more rare. No wonder the NSW Police could not get a handle on him.

Some of the most obvious clichés about police work are true. The first thirty days of an investigation *are* crucial. Most crimes are solved by *good, solid police work* by uniformed police. Most of the major leads in a case come from *outside* the investigation. Simply put, the Wanda Beach investigation went 'cold' because ordinary uniformed police officers from outside the circle of case detectives were not able to provide the leads that could be developed into the identification of a suspect.

And why did this happen? Incompetence? No. It was because of the absence of one intangible factor: luck … the policeman handing out a traffic ticket on Captain Cook Drive, the local sergeant supplying the name of a known sex offender, the parents reporting the disappearance of their son that Monday morning … the case never got the big break it needed, considering there was no suspect, eyewitness or weapon found. Over the years, there have been many false leads. In 1979 police questioned a 32-year-old Queensland man who had lived in Sydney in 1965 and matched the general description of one of the suspects. Sydney's *Daily Telegraph* splashed the news all over its 15 July front page, but there was no follow-up to the story; it was as if the big break the police finally had had disappeared overnight. Then there were the detectives who visited Margaret Kavazos at her home in the early 1980s to ask her about the son of a Lakemba fruit shop owner, but that was too far-fetched to be plausible. Members of the NSW State Parliament even invoked the memories of Christine Sharrock and Marianne Schmidt when they debated the Crimes (Forensic Procedures) Bill 2000, relating to the taking of bodily samples without consent. In June 2000 in the NSW Legislative Assembly, the Labor Party's Barry Collier (the Member for Miranda) took to the microphone:

I vividly recall at age fifteen being horrified when I heard that two young women of my age, Christine Sharrock and Marianne Schmidt, had been murdered at

Wanda Beach and their near-naked bodies had been buried in a shallow grave in sandhills among which the people of Sutherland Shire walked and engaged in recreational activities. The nation was shocked that two young women, who had gone to spend a day at the breach, would never return to their homes. The locals were shocked that the murder occurred at a place regularly frequented by them during the summer months … Now, thirty-five years on, this brutal crime remains unsolved. But, who knows, a DNA database for testing may be instrumental in bringing that culprit to justice.[11]

Today, the mere mention of the words 'Wanda Beach murders' is like a ghost tapping the public on the shoulder.

And an ending for this book? There are no happy endings regarding the deaths of Christine Sharrock and Marianne Schmidt — not for their families, their friends or the police who have spent five decades investigating their murders. There is no comfort in this, but perhaps the simplest explanation is true. The girls were in the wrong place at the wrong time. They did not plan to meet anyone at Wanda Beach on the day they died. On an impulse, they wandered off into the sandhills and met their deaths at the hands of an unknown killer. As Christine Sharrock's childhood friend said:

Today, I still stand firm that the girls didn't know their killer … This is what I've always believed. And I never imagined the person responsible being out on the streets. The thought of the Wanda Beach murderer marrying the girl next door, having kids and living happily ever after has never entered into my mind.

And I agree with her. I do not believe the murderer could

have gone home, showered and then put on another man's skin; there would be a continuing pattern of violence, abuse and perversion throughout his life. His demons would have consumed him and he would have slipped up the next time, or the time after that, and been caught. He would have had a wretched life, possibly spending time in prison for another crime in which he was not so fortunate to have hidden his tracks in the sand.

Perhaps he is long dead, shrouded in anonymity, and we have spent these past years chasing a phantom — someone who no longer exists.

On Monday, 11 January 1965, two fifteen-year-old friends met a horrifying death and were buried like jetsam in the sandhills at Wanda Beach. While the girls' memories now belong to history, Christine Sharrock and Marianne Schmidt deserve to be remembered as more than mere footnotes in a uniquely Australian episode of criminal history. And for that, the Wanda Beach murders deserve to be resolved.

Christine Sharrock and Marianne Schmidt rest uneasily until they are.

ENDNOTES

Chapter 1: The Last Days of Innocence
1. *Sun*, 21 January 1965.

Chapter 2: Monday, 11 January 1965
1. Police interview with Jeanette Taig, 13 January 1965.
2. All measurements are given in their original form. For conversion: 1 yd = 0.914 m; 1 ft = 30.5 cm; 1 in = 25.4 mm; 1 mile = 1.61 km; 1 lb = 454 g; 1 ton = 1.02 t; 1 in^2 = 6.45 cm^2; 1 ft^2 = 929 cm^2; $°C = 5/9 (°F–32)$; 1 stone = 6.35 kg.

Chapter 3: Christine and Marianne
1. As reproduced in official police documents, January 1965. Squarebracketed text is the author's addition, but all other parenthetical elements and asterisks are as they appeared in the police reproduction. The 'Chris' referred to in Marianne's diary is Christine Sharrock.
2. Information and quotes from the funeral services for Christine and Marianne were published in the *Sun*, 21 January 1965.

Chapter 4: The Crime Scene
1. Author's interview with Barry Ezzy, October 2002.
2. *Sun*, 20 January 1965.
3. 'Unsolved Murders: By the Sea', *Who Weekly*, 11 December 1995.
4. Author's interview with Steve Raymond, May 2003.

5. *Daily Mirror*, 13 January 1965.

Chapter 5: Media Wars

1. 'Pyjama Girl' case: On 3 September 1934, a woman's body, dressed only in pyjamas, was found hidden in a drain in the NSW southernborder town of Albury. When no one was able to identify the woman because of her injuries, police kept her body preserved in a bath of formaldehyde at Sydney University until her killer could be found. After a decade of being on display to the public, the woman was identified as Linda Agostini when her husband, Antonio, admitted to the murder.

2. 'Shark Arm' case: On Anzac Day (25 April) 1935, a shark caged in the Coogee Aquarium disgorged a human arm. After an intensive police investigation, the heavily tattooed arm was identified as belonging to James Smith, a member of the Sydney underworld. Smith was murdered as part of a gangland war but his killer was not identified.

3. 'Graeme Thorne kidnapping' case: On 1 June 1960, Bazil Thorne from Bondi in Sydney won £100,000 pounds in the NSW Opera House Lottery. On 7 July, the Thorne's seven-year-old son, Graeme, was kidnapped on his way to school. The Thornes had alerted police by the time a man with a thick European accent contacted them and demanded £25,000 for the boy's safe return. When Graeme Thorne's body was found six weeks later, police identified 38-year-old Stephen Bradley (a Hungarian immigrant, born Istvan Baranay) as the chief suspect. Bradley was later arrested in Ceylon and jailed for life.

4. Author's interviews with Margaret Kavazos, October and December 2002.

5. *Daily Mirror*, 19 January 1965.

6. 'Unsolved Murders: By the Sea', *Who Weekly*, 11 December 1995.

Chapter 6: Personal Pieces of the Puzzle

1. *Daily Mirror*, 13 January 1965.

2. 'Unsolved Murders: By the Sea', *Who Weekly*, 11 December 1995.

Chapter 7: The Police Investigation

1. *Daily Mirror*, 14 January 1965.

Chapter 8: Christine and Marianne Remembered

1. Police interview with Margaret Kavazos, 23 January 1965.
2. The remaining quotes from Margaret Kavazos come from her interviews with the author in October and December 2002.
3. Quotes from Elizabeth Schmidt (throughout the chapter) were published in the *Daily Mirror*, 8 January 1986.
4. Quotes from Norbert Schmidt (throughout the chapter) were published in the *Daily Mirror*, 9 January 1986.

Chapter 9: Possible Connections: Kruger and Dowlingkoa

1. Events in this chapter have been re-created from reports published in the *Illawarra Mercury* in 1966, as noted.
2. *Illawarra Mercury*, 23 September 1966.
3. *Illawarra Mercury*, 30 September 1966.
4. *Illawarra Mercury*, 31 September 1966.
5. *Illawarra Mercury*, 31 September 1966.
6. *Illawarra Mercury*, 30 September 1966.
7. 'Unsolved Murders: Serial Killer?', *Who Weekly*, 11 December 1995.
8. *Illawarra Mercury*, 1 February 1966.
9. *Illawarra Mercury*, 1 February 1966.
10. *Illawarra Mercury*, 30 September 1966.

Chapter 10: Cat and Mouse

1. Some events in this chapter have been re-created from various newspaper reports, as noted; other information comes from official police files.
2. Author's interview with Don Jones (former colleague of Cec Johnson), November 2002.
3. Details were published in the *Illawarra Mercury*, 24 September 1966.
4. *Illawarra Mercury*, 25 September 1966.
5. Details were published in the *Illawarra Mercury*, 26 July 1966.
6. *Illawarra Mercury*, 25 September 1966.
7. *Illawarra Mercury*, 31 September 1966.

8. *Illawarra Mercury*, 25 July 1966.

9. 'Unsolved Murders: By the Sea', *Who Weekly*, 11 December 1995.

10. The information regarding Johnson's interaction with Bassett and Bassett's family came from the author's interview with Don Jones, November 2002.

Chapter 11: Australian Psyche

1. Unless otherwise noted, details of the Beaumont case were re-created from the following media sources: 'Unsolved Murders: The Last Goodbye', *Who Weekly*, 11 December 1995; *Serial Killers: Christopher Wilder*, www.angelfire.com; Russell Brown, 'The Beaumont Children — At the Beach', 'The Beaumont Children — The Search', 'The Beaumont Children — The Psychic' and 'The Beaumont Children — False Hopes', all from www.beaumontchildren.com, 1999.

2. Norman Mailer, *The Time of Our Time*, Random House, New York, 1998.

3. (Wanda Beach investigation) police running sheet, 23 January 1965.

4. Stuart Coupe and Julie Ogden (ed), *Case Reopened*, Allen & Unwin, Sydney, 1993.

5. Dave Warner, *Big Bad Blood*, Random House, Sydney, 1997.

6. Bill Jenkins and Ian Heads, *As Crime Goes By*, Ironbark Press, Sydney, 1993.

7. *Sydney Morning Herald*, 14 June 1998.

8. *Sydney Morning Herald*, 22 April 1990.

9. *Sydney Morning Herald*, 4 June 1988.

Chapter 12: Antiquity

1. Both quotes from Margaret Kavazos come from her interviews with the author in October and December 2002.

2. Details of the Janine Balding case were published in the *Sydney Morning Herald*, 22 June 1990; the reference to DNA testing comes from the author's interview with Detective Inspector Russell Oxford, September 2002; the reference to improved DNA technology was published in the *Daily Telegraph*, 16 January 2003.

3. Patrick Bellamy, *Robert D. Keppel, Ph.D: An Interview with Patrick Bellamy*, The Crime Library, Dark Horse Multimedia, www.crimelibrary.com, 2000.

4. Patrick Bellamy, *Robert D. Keppel, Ph.D: An Interview with Patrick Bellamy*.

5. *Murder Casebook* (Vol. 1, No. 8), Gordon and Gotch, Australia, 1990.

6. Jakubowski, Maxim and Braund (eds), *The Mammoth Book of Jack the Ripper*, Constable & Robinson, London, 1999.

7. Ressler, Robert K, *Whoever Fights Monsters*, Simon & Schuster, New York 1993.

8. Beadle, William, 'The Real Jack the Ripper', *The Mammoth Book of Jack the Ripper*.

9. Beadle, William, 'The Real Jack the Ripper', *The Mammoth Book of Jack the Ripper*.

10. Patrick Bellamy, *Robert D. Keppel, Ph.D: An Interview with Patrick Bellamy*.

11. Official Hansard records of NSW State Government, 7 June 2000.

BIBLIOGRAPHY

'About DNA', Lakehead University, www.ancientdna.com.

Beadle, William, 'The Real Jack the Ripper', The Mammoth Book of Jack the Ripper, Constable & Robinson, London, 1999.

Bellamy, Patrick, Robert D. Keppel, Ph.D: An Interview by Patrick Bellamy, The Crime Library, Dark Horse Multimedia, www. crimelibrary.com, 2000.

Brown, Russell, 'The Beaumont Children — At the Beach', 'The Beaumont Children — The Search', 'The Beaumont Children — The Psychic' and 'The Beaumont Children — False Hopes', all from www. beaumontchildren.com, 1999.

'The Coogee Palace: The Shark Arm Case', www.randwick.nsw.gov.

Daily Mirror (various articles as quoted throughout the text)

Daily Telegraph (various articles as quoted throughout the text)

Department of Immigration, 'Immigration After World War II', www.immi.gov.au, accessed December 2002.

WANDA

Illawarra Mercury (various articles as quoted throughout the text)

Jakubowski, Maxim and Braund (eds), The Mammoth Book of Jack the Ripper, Constable & Robinson, London, 1999.

Kidd, Ross B, 'Famous Kidnappings: The Graeme Thorne Case', www.crimelibrary.com.

Mailer, Norman, The Time of Our Time, Random House, New York, 1998.

Murder Casebook (vols 4 and 8), Gordon & Gotch, Australia, 1990.

NSW Department of Health, About Schizophrenia (3rd ed), NSW Health Publication, 1990.

Official Legislative Assembly Hansard records [transcripts] of the NSW State Government, 7 June 2000, www.parliament.nsw.gov.au.

'The Pyjama Girl: Tours of Melbourne', www.whitehat.com.au.

Ressler, Robert K, Whoever Fights Monsters, Simon and Schuster, New York, 1993.

'Serial Killers: Christopher Wilder', www.angelfire.com.

Sun (various articles as quoted throughout the text)

'Unsolved Murders', Who Weekly, 11 December 1995.

Woffinden, Bob, 'Timothy Evans: Miscarriages of Justice', www. innocent.org.uk, 1987.